Philippians

Don Williams
Bill Gerrity

GL **Regal Books** A Division of G/L Publications
Glendale, California, U.S.A.

Other Good Regal Reading:
Philemon, Inductive Bible Study Series
  by Don Williams and Bill Gerrity
The Christian Life: Issues and Answers
  by Gary Maeder with Don Williams
The Apostle Paul and Women in the Church
  by Don Williams
The Bond that Breaks
  by Don Williams
Objections Answered
  by R.C. Sproul

The foreign language publishing of all Regal books is under the direction of *Gospel Literature International* (GLINT), a missionary assistance organization founded in 1961 by Dr. Henrietta C. Mears. Each year *Gospel Literature International* provides financial and technical help for the adaptation, translation and publishing of books and Bible study materials in more than 85 languages for millions of people worldwide.

For more information you are invited to write to *Gospel Literature International*, Glendale, California 91204.

Published by Regal Books Division, G/L Publications
Glendale, California 91209
Printed in U.S.A.

Library of Congress Catalog Card No. 79-64292
ISBN 0-8307-0704-2
Second Edition 1979

Previously published as *Journey into Joy*

Contents

Introduction

An Invitation to Inductive Bible Study

This invitation to Bible study is an invitation to high adventure: the adventure of hearing God speak above the clatter of human confusion and critique; the adventure of discovering truth for yourself; the adventure of seeing the Bible come alive in all of its richness as it stirs your imagination, stretches your mind and explodes in your heart.

The magic of this adventure is that you are the necessary ingredient, not as a passive reader but as an active, creative participant. We are about to have a dialogue with the Bible and with each other as you help write this study.

Think for a moment about what the Bible is *not*. It is not a sacred museum of bygone romantic heroes cloaked in "thees" and "thous." It *is* a living history of real people walking in the shadow as well as the light. They were born. They struggled with life. They questioned their identity. They doubted God. At times they went to war. They longed for peace. They felt oppression. They loved to eat. They married. They had sex. They prayed. And in the midst of the life they lived on the stark cruel desert or on a lonely mountain peak or in a great city, God spoke. Suddenly, the sky was filled with angels and God's Spirit broke into human hearts like a comet burning itself into the earth's crust.

The Bible is *not* simply a book for scholars and theologians trained in Hebrew, Greek, archaeology and exegesis. True, the Bible richly rewards these disciplines. It *is*, however, God's book for His people. While being fully human it is also fully divine. While it connects with our humanity, the same Spirit who indwelt its authors witnesses its divine truth to our hearts. Thus as we bring to the Bible our human nature, our unique experiences and our faith, we are met by the living God. After that encounter, scholarship may enhance study; before that, scholarship becomes a burden of technicalities which, like the middle ages, puts the Bible into Latin and chains it back into the cathedral. Luther said that every peasant having the Bible in his own language would be as good a theologian as the Pope. It is our hope that through this journey we will discover that the Bible is in *our* language and get turned on by that discovery.

What, then, do we need for serious Bible study?

A good modern literal translation. The *New American Standard Bible* is fine. Avoid the paraphrases such as *Good News Bible, Today's English Version* or the *Amplified Bible* or the *Living Bible.* We want to be as close to the original languages as a literal English translation can get us.

A lot of paper and pencils. We plan to write. We want to be free to mark our Bible, take notes, make comments. When I express my thoughts on paper they become *my thoughts.* Also, I remember much better and have something to share with others.

A place for serious, quiet study. Dr. Howard T. Kuist

says, "Bible study is rigorous business, and if it's not rigorous business to you, you haven't studied the Bible." There is a time for the simple devotional reading of God's Word and there is a time for *work*. We need to get ready for work, and I assure you that this work becomes exciting as we find the joy of discovery together.

An open, prayerful heart. The Bible promises that the Spirit of God will be our teacher. An attitude of receptivity, a waiting for God to speak, a patience bred by humility will position us as good listeners. "You do not have because you do not ask" (Jas. 4:2); "Ask and you will receive, that your joy may be made full" (John 16:24). So we come.

A group of fellow-adventurers. Personal study must lead to sharing with others. The Christian community is inherently corrective. When I go off on a tangent my companions bring me back. They enhance my thoughts, complement my insights and fill in what I overlook. The excitement of discovery must be shared. When my joy becomes your joy, we both grow. The Bible and our study are intensely relational as we hold each other to what God is teaching us and seek to live it out in our special worlds.

The Bible focuses supremely on one person: Jesus Christ. Since the Bible is the history of redemption, God's open heart to an alienated world, the key to its understanding is the Redeemer. Throughout the Old Testament a tension builds as Israel is promised things that she will eventually receive. Through many centuries of patriarchal example and prophetic Word, the little nation is prepared for the coming one. Finally, in mystery, the eternal Word of God takes upon our flesh and enters our history to make it one with Himself. This identification goes even unto death upon an execution hill outside Jerusalem. Time then stops as the pattern of our tired sorrow and grief is reversed in the Easter shout, "He is not here, He is risen."

To put it simply, to read the Bible is to read about Jesus: old covenant—new covenant; promise—fulfillment. This is the clue to its heartbeat. All else now falls into place. And the risen Redeemer, Jesus Himself, meets us through His Spirit to open our eyes on our Emmaus Way.

Before us in the New Testament are real *letters*. Does that capture your interest? It does mine. I love to get letters. When I was growing up I raced my sister hopefully to the mailbox each day looking for a letter. The only thing more exciting than reading your own mail is to read someone else's mail, and this is exactly what we are doing when we study Paul's letters. We are reading other people's mail.

It is important to realize this from the beginning because these letters are candid windows into first century Christianity. Here we find the drama of new life beginning to grow as it struggles with a hostile environment, works out internal problems and defines its faith. All this happens under the persuasive direction of one of history's geniuses—the apostle Paul.

OUR METHOD OF STUDY

We shall use what is called the inductive method of Bible study. By this we hope to draw from the Bible what is actually there to "induce" from the text its meaning, rather than to read our ideas or what scholars say into it. By this we also give God a chance to speak first. At last He can get beyond our favorite verses, often chosen by our needs, and confront us with His truth which, like the probe of a skilled doctor, only hurts to heal.

How does the inductive method work?

The inductive method is based on observation—seeing

and accounting for what is actually in the text. How often do we read over difficult or apparently uninteresting passages? How often do we pass over words we cannot define: *Propitiation* —"What's that?"; *Grace*— "Is that a girl's name or something you say before dinner?" Now, however, we force ourselves, in the words of the old railroad sign, to stop, look and listen.

The key to observation is learning to ask the right *questions:*

Why does Paul say this?

Why is this word here?

Why does he quote from the Old Testament?

Why is this sentence interrupted?

Why? Why? Why?

As we question the text, it gives up its answers. We must force ourselves to overlook *nothing;* no cop-outs. The creed of inductive Bible study is:

"I solemnly swear to read the whole text, and nothing but the text, so help me, please God."

As we *observe* the whole text, and *question* the text, it then determines our results and conclusions. Thus, the inductive method gets us to the heart of our faith. When Luther was called upon to retract his writings, he replied, "If you can show me from Scripture where I have erred, I will recant." We must be ready to do the same.

The inductive method takes each biblical book as an organic whole. Regardless of theories about its composition, the book before us is what we now have. Some books, such as Paul's letters, were written by one author over a brief period of time. Other books, like the Gospels, were edited from earlier materials. Regardless of how each one came together we now have the completed book before us and it must be studied in this form. This means that our first task is to read the book all the way through, to see it from beginning to end. Who would ever think of reading the first chapter of a detective story and then set out to analyze it without any regard for the outcome of the plot? Yet, we do this to the Bible again and again. It is true that each verse has meaning, but no verse stands alone. Each relates to the other and, ultimately, all relates to the whole Bible.

Words are the first basic unit of the text, but they mean something because of the order in which they are placed according to the laws of grammar. Phrases and clauses make up sentences. They, in turn, build paragraphs which connect to each other to make up the whole. As we watch all of this take place and ask why each word, sentence, and paragraph is where it is, we are beginning to take the Bible on its terms, and it will unfold for us.

A student of Louis Agassiz describes his first encounter with the inductive method in a biology class at Yale. Agassiz brought in a tin pan with a small fish in it. The student was to study it, without communicating with any other student or reading any books about fish. His job was to find out what he could about the fish, *from the fish*. After an hour the student felt finished, but Agassiz left him alone for a week. Dismayed, but challenged, the student spent 100 hours studying the fish. "I got interested in finding out how the scales went in series, their shape, the form and placement of the teeth, etc." At the end of the week Agassiz was still dissatisfied with the results. The student said, "In another week of ten hours a day labor, I had results which astonished myself and satisfied him. I shall never forget the sense of power which this experience brought me. I had learned the art of comparing objects." This is the inductive method: questioning and observing of the whole. Believe me, the Bible is more exciting than Agassiz's fish!

The inductive method of Bible study sees that each book came out of a specific historical context and begins

9

by establishing that context. Christians do not believe that the Bible dropped out of heaven, as do the Muslims about the Koran. The exciting thing about the God of the Bible is that He is a person who reveals Himself to persons in real time and space. Since God speaks and acts in history, as we understand the historical context of His revelation and the people through whom He has made Himself known, we understand more of Him. Our God is "the God of Abraham, Isaac and Jacob." He is known by His historical and personal relationships.

Thus, as we understand Judaism of the first century, we understand more of what Jesus faced. To reconstruct the position of the Pharisees from Matthew's Gospel, is to illumine the content of that Gospel. To know who Paul's opponents were in Galatia or Colossae is to see his letters to those churches come alive.

To summarize: The inductive method (1) observes and questions the text of the book to be studied; (2) sees all the elements of that text in relation to the whole; and (3) interprets the text in light of its historical context.

USING THE METHOD

We shall be using Paul's letter to the Philippians as our object of study. Our study will be thorough and will require a hearty effort, but to the diligent will go the rewards because in Philippians we discover the heartbeat of Christian joy.

As we said, we must first see Philippians as a whole letter in order to understand the interrelationship of its parts. Thus we begin by reading the letter all the way through in one sitting to get a proper sense of it. As in Agassiz's classroom, we begin by looking at the fish.

At the same time, we must seek to understand this letter in its historical context. As we read we ask: Why did Paul write it? What needs, issues, problems, or reasons motivated him?

Our assumption is that this letter is not just a random note written for no particular reason. My Aunt Nellie writes such notes. She tells the family when the sun rose, how many eggs the chickens laid and other such predictable news. When you have read one of her letters, you have read them all. Paul, however, was much too busy to write chatty letters. When he wrote, he had concrete reasons for writing and until we see them, we shall never get to the heart of his letters or to the way in which he put them together.

When a general sends his troops into battle he wants to win the war. He knows his goal, he knows his overall strategy, and he has his tactics—his individual moves—which become part of his battle plan. As Paul writes, then, he has his goal, his strategy and his tactics for accomplishing his goal. It is our job to discover all of this.

To determine Paul's purpose for writing and his strategy we must first determine his situation and the situation of the Philippians to whom he writes. Only after we understand this can we begin to study. In other words, when we know the historical context of the atmosphere out of which the letter has come, we can understand the letter itself. To return to Agassiz's fish, only when we understand that the fish comes out of the water and is made for the water can we begin to understand its function. Now the gills and fins make sense.

The one thing which we have is the letter. What we must recreate is the context out of which it has come. This means drawing from the text everything we can find out about Paul and everything we can find out about the Philippians.

Who is Paul? What is Paul's situation as he writes? What is his relationship to the Philippians? What motivates Paul to write this letter?

As we question the text, slowly the picture of Paul

emerges. We see a real man in a concrete historical situation writing the letter now before us.

At the same time we must ask: Who are the Philippians? What is their situation as Paul sees it? What is their previous relationship to Paul? Once again, a real church begins to emerge.

The relationship between Paul and the Philippians provides the atmosphere for his letter. As we recreate it in our minds, the Apostle's reason or reasons for writing will become clear. Knowing Paul's goals, we will then see his strategy and his tactics in reaching those goals, and this will engage us in a serious study of the letter.

Our method is simple:

1. Read Philippians all the way through and write a title or summary sentence for each paragraph.

2. Write down everything that you discover about Paul's situation and everything that you discover about the situation of the church.

3. Summarize all that you find out about Paul and all that you find out about the Philippians.

4. Summarize Paul's reasons for writing.

This will establish the Apostle's goals for this letter and prepare us to begin the study of the text. As Paul sits down to write, his mind is dominated by the needs of the church. This determines what and how he says it. Only when we understand this are we ready to study.

Since this guide is based upon the *New American Standard Bible*, the text is printed here for you. A space is provided before each paragraph for you to write in your summary title. The paragraphs have been shortened for more effective study. When you finish, compare your work with mine and see if you agree. If not, why not?

Introduction to Philippians

Philippians is a surprising letter. The young Christian movement is under attack. While the apostle Paul is locked up in a Roman dungeon, his church is faced with the suspicion that to be a Christian is to be subversive. Thus the authorities are preparing appropriate action. At the same time, internal conflicts threaten to split the congregation wide open and waves of false teaching beat against it. Here, then, is the surprise: In the midst of this Paul *rejoices*.

We too are faced with adversity. Circumstances seem to overwhelm us. Our mood easily reflects our times. Paul cries from his cell: "Rejoice!" We answer, "You must be an idiot, out of touch with reality, unaware of our situation. How can you tell us to rejoice when even the earth under our feet is giving way?" The Apostle responds, "I know the secret of life. Even in the midst of pain, joy prevails."

What is that secret? Our study in Philippians will unlock Paul's answer. The inductive method is the key. Here we stand on the threshold of a journey into joy.

CREATE PARAGRAPH TITLES
Philippians 1:1-30

*1:1 Title:*_____

   1   Paul and Timothy, bond-servants of Christ Jesus, to all the saints in Christ Jesus who are in Philippi, including the overseers and deacons:

*1:2 Title:*_____

   2   Grace to you and peace from God our Father and the Lord Jesus Christ.

*1:3-11 Title:*_____

   3   I thank my God in all my remembrance of you,

   4   always offering prayer with joy in my every prayer for you all,

   5   in view of your participation in the gospel from the first day until now.

   6   For I am confident of this very thing, that He who began a good work in you will perfect it until the day of Christ Jesus.

   7   For it is only right for me to feel this way about you all, because I have you in my heart, since both in my imprisonment and in the defense and confirmation of the gospel, you all are partakers of grace with me.

   8   For God is my witness, how I long for you all with the affection of Christ Jesus.

   9   And this I pray, that your love may abound still more and more in real knowledge and all discernment,

   10   so that you may approve the things that are excellent, in order to be sincere and blameless until the day of Christ;

11 having been filled with the fruit of righteousness which comes through Jesus Christ, to the glory and praise of God.

1:12-14 Title:_____
12 Now I want you to know, brethren, that my circumstances have turned out for the greater progress of the gospel,

13 so that my imprisonment in the cause of Christ has become well-known throughout the whole praetorian guard and to everyone else,

14 and that most of the brethren, trusting in the Lord because of my imprisonment, have far more courage to speak the word of God without fear.

1:15-18 Title:_____
15 Some, to be sure, are preaching Christ even from envy and strife, but some also from good will;

16 the latter do it out of love, knowing that I am appointed for the defense of the gospel;

17 the former proclaim Christ out of selfish ambition, rather than from pure motives, thinking to cause me distress in my imprisonment.

18 What then? Only that in every way, whether in pretense or in truth, Christ is proclaimed; and in this I rejoice, yes, and I will rejoice.

1:19-26 Title:_____
19 For I know that this shall turn out for my deliverance through your prayers and the provision of the Spirit of Jesus Christ,

20 according to my earnest expectation and hope, that I shall not be put to shame in anything, but that with all boldness, Christ shall even now, as always, be exalted in my body, whether by life or by death.

21 For to me, to live is Christ, and to die is gain.

22   But if I am to live on in the flesh, this will mean fruitful labor for me; and I do not know which to choose.

23   But I am hard pressed from both directions, having the desire to depart and be with Christ, for that is very much better;

24   yet to remain on in the flesh is more necessary for your sake.

25   And convinced of this, I know that I shall remain and continue with you all for your progress and joy in the faith,

26   so that your proud confidence in me may abound in Christ Jesus through my coming to you again.

1:27-30 Title:_____

27   Only conduct yourselves in a manner worthy of the gospel of Christ; so that whether I come and see you or remain absent, I may hear of you that you are standing firm in one spirit, with one mind striving together for the faith of the gospel;

28   in no way alarmed by your opponents—which is a sign of destruction for them, but of salvation for you, and that too, from God.

29   For to you it has been granted for Christ's sake, not only to believe in Him, but also to suffer for His sake,

30   experiencing the same conflict which you saw in me, and now hear to be in me.

Philippians 2:1-30

2:1-11 Title:_____

1   If therefore there is any encouragement in Christ, if there is any consolation of love, if there is any fellowship of the Spirit, if any affection and compassion,

2   make my joy complete by being of the same mind, maintaining the same love, united in spirit, intent on one purpose.

3   Do nothing from selfishness or empty conceit, but with humility of mind let each of you regard one another as more important than himself;

4   do not merely look out for your own personal interests, but also for the interests of others.

5   Have this attitude in yourselves which was also in Christ Jesus,

6   who, although He existed in the form of God, did not regard equality with God a thing to be grasped,

7   but emptied Himself, taking the form of a bond-servant, and being made in the likeness of men.

8   And being found in appearance as a man, He humbled Himself by becoming obedient to the point of death, even death on a cross.

9   Therefore also God highly exalted Him, and bestowed on Him the name which is above every name,

10   that at the name of Jesus every knee should bow, of those who are in heaven, and on earth, and under the earth,

11   and that every tongue should confess that Jesus Christ is Lord, to the glory of God the Father.

2:12,13 Title:_____

12   So then, my beloved, just as you have always obeyed, not as in my presence only, but now much more in my absence, work out your salvation with fear and trembling;

13   for it is God who is at work in you, both to will and to work for His good pleasure.

2:14-18 Title:_____

14   Do all things without grumbling or disputing;

15   that you may prove yourselves to be blameless and innocent, children of God above reproach in the midst of a crooked and perverse generation, among whom you appear as lights in the world,

16   holding fast the word of life, so that in the day of Christ I may have cause to glory because I did not run in vain nor toil in vain.

17   But even if I am being poured out as a drink offering upon the sacrifice and service of your faith, I rejoice and share my joy with you all.

18   And you too, I urge you, rejoice in the same way and share your joy with me.

2:19-24 Title: _____

19   But I hope in the Lord Jesus to send Timothy to you shortly, so that I also may be encouraged when I learn of your condition.

20   For I have no one else of kindred spirit who will genuinely be concerned for your welfare.

21   For they all seek after their own interests, not those of Christ Jesus.

22   But you know of his proven worth that he served with me in the furtherance of the gospel like a child serving his father.

23   Therefore I hope to send him immediately, as soon as I see how things go with me;

24   and I trust in the Lord that I myself also shall be coming shortly.

2:25-30 Title: _____

25   But I thought it necessary to send to you Epaphroditus, my brother and fellow-worker and fellow-soldier, who is also your messenger and minister to my need;

26   because he was longing for you all and was distressed because you had heard that he was sick.

27   For indeed he was sick to the point of death, but God had mercy on him, and not on him only but also on me, lest I should have sorrow upon sorrow.

28   Therefore I have sent him all the more eagerly in

order that when you see him again you may rejoice and I may be less concerned about you.

29 Therefore receive him in the Lord with all joy, and hold men like him in high regard;

30 because he came close to death for the work of Christ, risking his life to complete what was deficient in your service to me.

Philippians 3:1-21

3:1 Title: _____

1 Finally, my brethren, rejoice in the Lord. To write the same things again is no trouble to me, and it is a safeguard for you.

3:2-11 Title: _____

2 Beware of the dogs, beware of the evil workers, beware of the false circumcision;

3 for we are the true circumcision, who worship in the Spirit of God and glory in Christ Jesus and put no confidence in the flesh,

4 although I myself might have confidence even in the flesh. If anyone else has a mind to put confidence in the flesh, I far more:

5 circumcised the eighth day, of the nation of Israel, of the tribe of Benjamin, a Hebrew of Hebrews, as to the Law, a Pharisee;

6 as to zeal, a persecutor of the church, as to the righteousness which is in the Law, found blameless.

7 But whatever things were gain to me, those things I have counted as loss for the sake of Christ.

8 More than that, I count all things to be loss in view of the surpassing value of knowing Christ Jesus my Lord, for whom I have suffered the loss of all things, and count them but rubbish in order that I may gain Christ,

9 and may be found in Him, not having a righteous-

ness of my own derived from the Law, but that which is through faith in Christ, the righteousness which comes from God on the basis of faith,

10   that I may know Him, and the power of His resurrection and the fellowship of His sufferings, being conformed to His death;

11   in order that I may attain to the resurrection from among the dead.

3:12-16 Title: _____

12   Not that I have already obtained it, or have already become perfect, but I press on in order that I may lay hold of that for which also I was laid hold of by Christ Jesus.

13   Brethren, I do not regard myself as having laid hold of it yet; but one thing I do: forgetting what lies behind and reaching forward to what lies ahead,

14   I press on toward the goal for the prize of the upward call of God in Christ Jesus.

15   Let us therefore, as many as are perfect, have this attitude; and if in anything you have a different attitude, God will reveal that also to you;

16   however, let us keep living by that same standard to which we have attained.

3:17-21 Title: _____

17   Brethren, join in following my example, and observe those who walk according to the pattern you have in us.

18   For many walk, of whom I often told you, and now tell you even weeping, that they are enemies of the cross of Christ,

19   whose end is destruction, whose god is their appetite, and whose glory is in their shame, who set their minds on earthly things.

20   For our citizenship is in heaven, from which also

we eagerly wait for a Savior, the Lord Jesus Christ;

21   who will transform the body of our humble state into conformity with the body of His glory, by the exertion of the power that He has even to subject all things to Himself.

Philippians 4:1-23

*4:1 Title:*_____

1   Therefore, my beloved brethren whom I long to see, my joy and crown, so stand firm in the Lord, my beloved.

*4:2,3 Title:*_____

2   I urge Euodia and I urge Syntyche to live in harmony in the Lord.

3   Indeed, true comrade, I ask you also to help these women who have shared my struggle in the cause of the gospel, together with Clement also, and the rest of my fellow-workers, whose names are in the book in life.

*4:4-7 Title:*_____

4   Rejoice in the Lord always; again I will say, rejoice!

5   Let your forbearing spirit be known to all men. The Lord is near.

6   Be anxious for nothing, but in everything by prayer and supplication with thanksgiving let your requests be made known to God.

7   And the peace of God, which surpasses all comprehension, shall guard your hearts and your minds in Christ Jesus.

*4:8,9 Title:*_____

8   Finally, brethren, whatever is true, whatever is honorable, whatever is right, whatever is pure, whatever is lovely, whatever is of good repute, if there is any excel-

lence and if anything worthy of praise, let your mind dwell on these things.

9 The things you have learned and received and heard and seen in me, practice these things; and the God of peace shall be with you.

4:10-13 Title:_____

10 But I rejoiced in the Lord greatly, that now at last you have revived your concern for me; indeed, you were concerned before, but you lacked opportunity.

11 Not that I speak from want; for I have learned to be content in whatever circumstances I am.

12 I know how to get along with humble means, and I also know how to live in prosperity; in any and every circumstance I have learned the secret of being filled and going hungry, both of having abundance and suffering need.

13 I can do all things through Him who strengthens me.

4:14-20 Title:_____

14 Nevertheless, you have done well to share with me in my affliction.

15 And you yourselves also know, Philippians, that at the first preaching of the gospel, after I departed from Macedonia, no church shared with me in the matter of giving and receiving but you alone;

16 for even in Thessalonica you sent a gift more than once for my needs.

17 Not that I seek the gift itself, but I seek for the profit which increases to your account.

18 But I have received everything in full, and have an abundance; I am amply supplied, having received from Epaphroditus what you have sent, a fragrant aroma, an acceptable sacrifice, well pleasing to God.

19 And my God shall supply all your needs accord-

ing to His riches in glory in Christ Jesus.

20   *Now to our God and Father be the glory forever and ever. Amen.*

4:21,22 Title:_____
21   *Greet every saint in Christ Jesus. The brethren who are with me greet you.*

22   *All the saints greet you, especially those of Caesar's household.*

4:23 Title:_____
23   *The grace of the Lord Jesus Christ be with your spirit.*

MY PARAGRAPH TITLES

Now compare your work with mine.

1:1: Paul and Timothy greet the Christians and their leaders at Philippi.

1:2: Paul gives them a blessing of grace and peace.

1:3-11: Paul thanks God for their participation in the gospel and prays for their maturity.

1:12-14: Paul's imprisonment advances the gospel inside and outside.

1:15-18: The preaching of Christ makes him happy regardless of motives.

1:19-26: Paul stands between life and death—all is for Christ.

1:27-30: The Philippians must be together to stand against their enemies.

2:1-11: Christ offers the resources and is the model for Christian unity.

2:12,13: We work because God is at work.

2:14-18: Exhortation to steadfastness even if Paul is sacrificed.

2:19-24: Timothy will visit the Philippians and Paul hopes to follow.

23

2:25-30: Epaphroditus, having served Paul, will now return.
3:1: Rejoice!
3:2-11: Paul's life in Judaism and in Christ.
3:12-16: Press on to the goal as Paul does.
3:17-21: Warning against license.
4:1: Stand firm.
4:2,3: A call to reconciliation for Euodia and Syntyche.
4:4-7: Rejoice through prayer and find peace.
4:8,9: Think about the best, follow Paul's example.
4:10-13: The secret of contentment.
4:14-20: Thanks for the Philippians' gift of money.
4:21,22: Farewell greetings.
4:23: Benediction of grace.

THE HISTORICAL CONTEXT

Now we are ready to gather the evidence for Paul's situation and that of the Philippians. Go through the letter again and jot down the raw materials which you find for each. I have written in the answers to verse 1 to demonstrate our task. Compare your work with mine in the next section after you are through.

Paul	The Philippians
1:1 A servant of Christ with Timothy.	1:1 Saints living in Philippi. Organized with overseers and deacons.
1:3	
	1:5
1:7	1:7
1:8	
	1:9

24

Paul	The Philippians
1:12	
1:13	
1:14	
1:15,16	
1:17	
1:18	
1:19	1:19
1:20	
1:22	
1:23	
1:24	
1:25	
1:26	
1:27	
	1:28
	1:29
1:30	1:30
2:2	
	2:12

Paul	The Philippians
2:16	
2:17	
2:19	
2:20	
2:22	
2:23	
2:24	
2:25	2:25
	2:26
2:27	
2:28	
2:30	
3:1	
	3:2
3:3	
3:4	
3:5	
3:6	

Paul	The Philippians
3:7	
3:8	
3:12	
3:13	
3:14	
3:15	
3:17	3:17
3:18	3:18
4:1	
	4:2
4:3	4:3
4:9	
4:10	4:10
4:11	
4:12	
	4:14
4:15	4:15
	4:16

Paul	The Philippians
4:18	4:18
4:21	
4:22	

Now compare your work with mine:

Paul	The Philippians
1:1 A servant of Christ with Timothy.	*1:1* Saints living in Philippi. Organized with overseers and deacons.
1:3 Paul is thankful to God for the Philippians.	*1:5* Participants in the gospel from their conversion to the present.
1:7 Holds the Philippians in his heart as he is in prison for the gospel. *1:8* Longs for the Philippians.	*1:7* They are partakers of grace with Paul in his defense and confirmation of the gospel. *1:9* Loving.
1:12 The gospel has progressed through Paul. *1:13* Shares his faith with the praetorian guard and all the rest. He is in prison for Christ. *1:14* His example encourages other Christians giving courage. *1:15* Mixed motives in evangelism. *1:16* Paul is appointed for	

28

the defense of the gospel.

1:17 Some seek to cause him distress.

1:18 Rejoices when Christ is proclaimed.

1:19 Hopes to be delivered.   *1:19* Pray for Paul

1:20 Hopes to exalt Christ regardless of the outcome.

1:22 To live means fruitful labor; but uncertain whether he would live or die.

1:23 Would rather be with Christ.

1:24 Necessary to remain for the Philippians.

1:25 Confident he will remain with them for their growth.

1:26 Hopes to come to them again.

1:27 Hopes to hear of their unity in his presence or absence.

1:28 Have opponents.

1:29 Are suffering persecution.

1:30 Experiencing conflict.   *1:30* Experiencing conflict and now hear of it in Paul.

2:2 Joy completed by the unity of the Philippians.

2:12 Obeyed in Paul's presence.

2:16 Hopes to glory be-
cause of the Philippians
when Christ returns.

2:17 Glad to be poured out
for them.

2:19 Hopes to send Timothy to them to return to him
with good news.

2:20 Timothy is unique in
his genuine concern.

2:22 Timothy has been like
a child to him.

2:23 Timothy will come
when his case is decided.

2:24 He hopes to visit the
church.

2:25 Epaphroditus has
been their messenger
and minister to Paul.

2:25 Epaphroditus is
his fellow-worker and
now returning.

2:26 Heard Epaphrodi-
tus was sick.

2:27 God's mercy on Paul
meant Epaphroditus' heal-
ing.

2:28 Eager to send Epaphroditus.

2:30 Epaphroditus com-
pleted their service to Paul.

3:1 Writes the same things
again.

3:2 Danger from false
teachers: Dogs, evil
workers, the false cir-
cumcision.

3:3 Spiritual life means no

confidence in the flesh.

3:4 Has the most reasons for confidence in the flesh.

3:5 Circumcised, Jew, tribe of Benjamin, Pharisee.

3:6 Persecuted the church, obeyed the law.

3:7 Gave up all for Christ.

3:8 Lost all for Christ.

3:12 Not perfect, presses on.

3:13 Forgets the past.

3:14 Presses on.

3:15 Perfect.

3:17 Some live as Paul lived.

3:17 Life an example for imitation.

3:18 Danger from the enemies of Christ's cross.

3:18 Repeats warnings, weeps.

4:1 Loves the church and longs for it.

4:2 Euodia and Syntyche called to agree.

4:3 "True comrade" must help these women who worked with Paul and Clement and others.

4:3 Euodia, Syntyche, Clement and others worked beside him for Christ.

4:9 Life is an example for the church.

4:10 Revived their concern for Paul

4:10 Happy over their concern

4:11 Content in any circumstances

4:12 Copes with all circumstances.

4:14 Share in Paul's trouble.

31

Paul	The Philippians
4:15 Partners with Paul from their conversion.	*4:15* Supported by the Philippians.
	4:16 Sent gifts to Paul in Thessalonica.
4:18 Sent gift to Paul with Epaphroditus.	*4:18* Received full payment from Epaphroditus.
	4:21 Brethren with Paul.
	4:22 Saints in Caesar's household.

Now, using the raw materials, summarize Paul's and the Philippians' situations:

Paul

The Philippians

Compare your summaries with mine:

Paul

Paul is a Jew who was circumcised on the eighth day (3:5). From the tribe of Benjamin, he interpreted the law as a Pharisee (3:5), fulfilling its demands (3:6); he persecuted the Christians (3:6). All of this accomplishment he gave up to know Christ (3:8).

Paul's service of Christ brought him to Philippi where he founded the church (1:5; 4:15) in the midst of persecution (1:30). Timothy was probably with him (1:1; 2:22).

Now he is in prison (1:7) where he continues his evangelistic efforts (1:12,13). As a result there are saints in Caesar's household (4:22). The Christians have also been encouraged in their witness by Paul's example (1:14), although not all preach Christ from proper motives (1:15-18).

Paul now faces the alternatives of life or death (1:20). He hopes to be delivered to continue to aid the Philippians (1:19,24). He would, however, rather depart and be with Christ (1:23).

Epaphroditus has come to Paul from Philippi bearing a gift of money (2:25,30; 4:14-18). He became ill and nearly died on the way but is now recovered and returning home (2:26-28).

Timothy will also visit the Philippians as soon as Paul's trial is completed (2:23). He has been a child to Paul, and genuinely cares for the church (2:19-22). The Apostle himself hopes to visit when released (1:27; 2:24).

Paul loves and longs for the Philippians (1:8; 4:1). He has companions in the church who have served Christ with him (4:3).

Forgetting the past (3:13), Paul presses on (3:14), offering his life as an example of Christian maturity (3:17), content in any state in which he is found (4:11, 12).

The Philippians

The Philippians are Christians (1:1) who were evangelized by Paul (1:5). Their response to the gospel has meant loyalty to the Apostle demonstrated by their financial support of his mission (4:15). They sent funds more than once to Thessalonica (4:16) and continued their aid when Paul left Macedonia (4:15). Now they have sent gifts again to him in prison through Epaphroditus (2:25; 4:18).

The church is organized with overseers and deacons (1:1). The Christians are loving (1:9) and praying (1:19). They are, however, in danger of division because of Euodia and Syntyche who Paul urges to live in harmony (4:2). "True comrade" is to reconcile these women (4:3).

The state is also threatening the church with the same kind of persecution Paul experienced in Philippi (1:30) and false teachers may undermine the gospel (3:2). Since the old life in the world is also attractive, the Philippians are tempted to return to it (3:18).

Hearing of Epaphroditus's illness, the Philippians have been worried about him and show their concern (2:26). Along with his return, they will be strengthened by Timothy whom they know and trust (2:22) while they expect Paul's release and arrival (1:19,25,26; 2:24).

In the meantime they are to follow the example of those in their midst who live like Paul, and imitate the Apostle as well (3:17).

What then, are Paul's reasons for writing?

Compare your results with mine:

Paul writes the Philippians to prepare them for persecution from without, to heal their division within, to warn them of false teachers, to guard them from returning to their old pagan ways, to thank them for their gift of money, and to commend Epaphroditus and Timothy to them.

In all of this the Apostle expresses his warm affection for the church and his joy over their sharing in the gospel.

A STRUCTURAL OVERVIEW OF PHILIPPIANS

This letter is dominated by example. In chapter 1 Paul presents his own in prison. In chapter 2 he recalls that of Christ. In chapter 3 he appeals to his own Christian experience. In chapter 4 he speaks of his attitude in diverse circumstances. Here is learning by example.

We may diagram Philippians as follows:

Chapter 1	Chapter 2	Chapter 3	Chapter 4
Salutation and prayer: 1:1-11 _____ *Persecution* The example of Paul, exhortation:1:12-30	*Division* The example of Christ, exhortation: 2:1-18 _____ Timothy and Epaphroditus: 2:17-30	*Heresy* The example of Paul vs. legalism and license: 3:1—4:1	Euodia, Syntyche, "True comrade," Clement:4:2,3 _____ *Thanksgiving* Prayer Attitudes Triumph Financial aid Farewell: 4:4-23

Notice that the letter breaks easily into two sections, chapters 1—2 and chapters 3—4. Each concludes with a personal appeal and instruction: Timothy and Epaphroditus are mentioned in 2:19-30 and Euodia, Syntyche, "True comrade," Clement, Paul and Epaphroditus all appear in chapter 4.

Now we are ready to study the text.

As we turn to the letter itself we will use six questions to uncover its meaning.

The language question deals with vocabulary. What is the meaning of each word? If you cannot supply a simple, clear definition, look it up in a regular dictionary or Bible dictionary.

This question also deals with *style*—is it poetry or prose? Is it a letter or proverb or parable? How is it being said? What is the sentence structure? Why are these words chosen? Where do they appear in the context?

The historical question deals with the setting of the text and its historical content. Who is speaking or acting? What is being said of an historical nature? When is it happening? We have already dealt with this question at length in our previous study. This will be just a review.

The theological question deals with theological content. What truths are taught about the nature of God, man, sin, salvation, the church, the Christian life, etc.? How can we understand them systematically?

The tactical question deals with where a particular paragraph or idea fits in light of Paul's reasons for writing. A military metaphor explains this. A commander creates a strategy and uses tactics to form his battle plan in winning a war. A coach creates a game plan to use his team effectively with the proper plays to win the game. A cook follows ordered steps in a recipe to reach the goal of a perfect cake. So Paul uses tactics in accomplishing his goals in writing this letter, and we want to see *how* he does this—how one idea leads to the next in reaching the goal.

The contemporary question deals with the application of the text to our world today. How do we apply what Paul said to government, politics, economics, business, education, the institutional church, the assumptions, values, and goals of our society?

The personal question deals with the application of the text to our own lives today. How do we relate what Paul said to our own personalities, needs, families, close friends, moral decisions, goals, etc.? What am I going to do about what I have learned?

In Part I we shall apply these questions to Philippians. If one does not fit a particular paragraph, leave it blank. In this type of study we are not forced to write something for each question if the paragraph does not yield it. Using the study sheets that follow read the text and the instructions or questions and respond in the space provided. You can either make up your own questions or use the specific ones provided under each paragraph from Philippians. You can then check your work with the commentary in Part II. It is best to do your own work first so that you come freely to the text. If you find a word you can't define when doing the language question you may look it up in the appropriate place in the commentary. Most of the theological words are defined in the vocabulary section there. Pray for the help of the Holy Spirit as you study.

Where you disagree with the commentary, great! Go back to the text again. You will have insights that others don't have. The question *always* is: What does the text say and mean? These inductive questions are to be used to open up the Scripture to our careful observation.

If you do not care to do your own study, you can read the commentary for upbuilding and devotional purposes. Come now and the growth will begin.

Part I

Inductive Bible Study
of Philippians

INDUCTIVE QUESTIONS FOR PHILIPPIANS 1:1

Paul and Timothy, bond-servants of Christ Jesus, to all the saints in Christ Jesus who are in Philippi, including the overseers and deacons:

Language

Vocabulary: Define *bond-servant; saints; overseers; deacons.*

Historical

What do you learn about Paul?
What do you learn about the church?

Theological

What does it mean to be a bond-servant of Christ?

Tactical

Why does Paul use the word "all" in light of the problem of division in Philippi?

Contemporary

What does it mean for Christians to be called "saints" in the world today?

What do most people think when they hear the word?

Personal

What does it mean for me to be a bond-servant of Jesus Christ?

INDUCTIVE QUESTIONS FOR PHILIPPIANS 1:2

Grace to you and peace from God our Father and the Lord Jesus Christ.

Language

a. *Vocabulary:* Define *grace* and *peace*.
   What does it mean to call God "Father"?

b. *Style:* What is the form of this verse?

Historical

Theological

What does this verse tell me about the relationship between God the Father and Jesus Christ?

Tactical

How does this verse provide the ground for Paul's relationship to the Philippians?

Contemporary

Where does the world look for peace today?

Personal

Where have I found peace?

INDUCTIVE QUESTIONS FOR PHILIPPIANS 1:3-11

3 *I thank my God in all my remembrance of you,*

4 *always offering prayer with joy in my every prayer for you all,*

5 *in view of your participation in the gospel from the first day until now.*

6 *For I am confident of this very thing, that He who began a good work in you will perfect it until the day of Christ Jesus.*

7 *For it is only right for me to feel this way about you all, because I have you in my heart, since both in my imprisonment and in the defense and confirmation of the gospel, you all are partakers of grace with me.*

8 *For God is my witness, how I long for you all with the affection of Christ Jesus.*

9 *And this I pray, that your love may abound still more and more in real knowledge and all discernment,*

10 *so that you may approve the things that are excellent, in order to be sincere and blameless until the day of Christ;*

11 *having been filled with the fruit of righteousness which comes through Jesus Christ, to the glory and praise of God.*

Language

a. *Vocabulary:* Define *the day of Christ Jesus; love; knowledge; discernment; sincere; blameless; the fruit of righteousness.*

b. *Style:* What are the parts of this prayer?

Historical

What do you learn here about Paul's situation and that of the church?

Theological

What is the meaning of the promise in 1:6?
What is the meaning of the order in which Paul prays for the church in 1:9-11?

Tactical

How are the specific issues in Philippi addressed in this prayer?

Contemporary

What is Paul's vision for the church and how is this reflected in our congregations?

Personal

How do my prayers measure up to Paul's?

INDUCTIVE QUESTIONS FOR PHILIPPIANS 1:12-14

12   Now I want you to know, brethren, that my circumstances have turned out for the greater progress of the gospel,

13   so that my imprisonment in the cause of Christ has become well-known throughout the whole praetorian guard and to everyone else,

14   and that most of the brethren, trusting in the Lord because of my imprisonment, have far more courage to speak the word of God without fear.

Language

Vocabulary: Define *gospel; praetorian guard; Word of God.*

Historical

What do you learn about those around Paul?

What do you learn about those on the outside?

Theological

How does God work through circumstances?

How is the gospel spread?

What does it mean to witness for Christ?

Tactical

How would these verses encourage the Philippians if they also are to be imprisoned for their faith?

Contemporary

What answer do we have for people who feel trapped by circumstances?

Personal

How am I responding to the adversity in my life?

What advantage do I take to influence people around me for Christ?

INDUCTIVE QUESTIONS FOR PHILIPPIANS 1:15-18

15   Some, to be sure, are preaching Christ even from envy and strife, but some also from good will;

16   the latter do it out of love, knowing that I am appointed for the defense of the gospel;

17   the former proclaim Christ out of selfish ambition, rather than from pure motives, thinking to cause me distress in my imprisonment.

18   What then? Only that in every way, whether in pretense or in truth, Christ is proclaimed; and in this I rejoice, yes, and I will rejoice.

Language

a. *Vocabulary:* Define *rejoice.*

b. *Style:* How does Paul contrast the two groups here?

Historical

What do you learn about the double response to Paul's imprisonment? Define each group.

What do you learn about Paul's attitude?

Theological

What is the Christian attitude toward mixed motives among people in serving Christ?

Why should we have such an attitude?

Tactical

How would these verses encourage the Philippians in facing persecution?

Contemporary

How can we help to heal division in the Body of Christ?

Personal

How do I react to other Christian motives?

INDUCTIVE QUESTIONS FOR PHILIPPIANS 1:19-26

19   For I know that this shall turn out for my deliverance through your prayers and the provision of the Spirit of Jesus Christ,

20   according to my earnest expectation and hope, that I shall not be put to shame in anything, but that with all boldness, Christ shall even now, as always, be exalted in my body, whether by life or by death.

21   For to me, to live is Christ, and to die is gain.

22   But if I am to live on in the flesh, this will mean fruitful labor for me; and I do not know which to choose.

23   But I am hard pressed from both directions, having the desire to depart and be with Christ, for that is very much better;

24   yet to remain on in the flesh is more necessary for your sake.

25   And convinced of this, I know that I shall remain and continue with you all for your progress and joy in the faith,

26   so that your proud confidence in me may abound in Christ Jesus through my coming to you again.

Language

a. *Vocabulary:* Define *the Spirit of Jesus Christ; the flesh; joy.*

b. *Style:* What key words appear here?
What are the basic contrasts?
What is the mood of this paragraph?

Historical

What do you learn here about Paul?
What do you learn about the Philippians?

Theological

How does Paul face death?
What is the meaning of life for Paul? Why?

Tactical

How would these verses help the Philippians face death for Christ?

Contemporary

How does our culture deal with death?
What is the Christian response?

Personal

What is life for me?

What are my honest feelings about death?

INDUCTIVE QUESTIONS FOR PHILIPPIANS 1:27-30

27   *Only conduct yourselves in a manner worthy of the gospel of Christ; so that whether I come and see you or remain absent, I may hear of you that you are standing firm in one spirit, with one mind striving together for the faith of the gospel;*

28   *in no way alarmed by your opponents—which is a sign of destruction for them, but of salvation for you, and that too, from God.*

29   *For to you it has been granted for Christ's sake, not only to believe in Him, but also to suffer for His sake,*

30   *experiencing the same conflict which you saw in me, and now hear to be in me.*

Language

Vocabulary: Define *salvation; suffer.*

Historical

What do you learn here about Paul?

What do you learn about the Philippians?

Theological

How are Christians to live worthy of the gospel of Christ?

What are the signs of a true Christian?

Tactical

How would these verses help the Philippians face suffering?

Contemporary

What does it mean today for the church to suffer for her faith?

Personal

How is my life worthy of the gospel?

Who are my opponents? How am I suffering for Christ?

INDUCTIVE QUESTIONS FOR PHILIPPIANS 2:1-11

1 If therefore there is any encouragement in Christ, if there is any consolation of love, if there is any fellowship of the Spirit, if any affection and compassion,

2 make my joy complete by being of the same mind, maintaining the same love, united in spirit, intent on one purpose.

3 Do nothing from selfishness or empty conceit, but with humility of mind let each of you regard one another as more important than himself;

4 do not merely look out for your own personal interests, but also for the interests of others.

5 Have this attitude in yourselves which was also in Christ Jesus,

6 who, although He existed in the form of God, did not regard equality with God a thing to be grasped,

7 but emptied Himself, taking the form of a bond-servant, and being made in the likeness of men.

8 And being found in appearance as a man, He humbled Himself by becoming obedient to the point of death, even death on a cross.

9 Therefore also God highly exalted Him, and bestowed on Him the name which is above every name,

10 that at the name of Jesus every knee should bow, of those who are in heaven, and on earth, and under the earth,

11 and that every tongue should confess that Jesus Christ is Lord, to the glory of God the Father.

Language

a. *Vocabulary:* Define *affection; mind; conceit; humility; form; under the earth; Lord.*

b. *Style:* What words and concepts are repeated?
What emphasis do the repetitions give?
What mood does the passage convey?

Historical

What is learned about Paul's relationship to the Philippians?

Theological

What does this passage say about Christ?
What is the attitude of Christ?
What does it mean to have the attitude of Christ?

Tactical

How do these verses address what was going on in Philippi?

Contemporary

Would this passage be meaningful if written to the church today? Why?

Personal

What experience have you had trying to be a Christ-like servant? What are the difficulties?

INDUCTIVE QUESTIONS FOR PHILIPPIANS 2:12,13

12 So then, my beloved, just as you have always obeyed, not as in my presence only, but now much more in my absence, work out your salvation with fear and trembling;

13 for it is God who is at work in you, both to will and to work for His good pleasure.

Language

a. *Vocabulary:* Define *beloved; to will.*

b. *Style:* What are the contrasts in this passage?
   What does "so then" indicate?

Historical
What is revealed about Paul's relationship with the Philippians?

Theological
In verse 12 how would the meaning change if Paul had said "work for" instead of "work out" your salvation?
According to these verses what is man to do?
What has God done?
How do these two functions work together?

Tactical
How would these verses help the Philippians to deal with their problems?

Contemporary
Are there groups today that stress the work of man and ignore the power of God?
Or some that emphasize God and forget man? Give some examples.

Personal

How do you work out your own salvation?

INDUCTIVE QUESTIONS FOR PHILIPPIANS 2:14-18

14   Do all things without grumbling or disputing;

15   that you may prove yourselves to be blameless and innocent, children of God above reproach in the midst of a crooked and perverse generation, among whom you appear as lights in the world,

16   holding fast the word of life, so that in the day of Christ I may have cause to glory because I did not run in vain nor toil in vain.

17   But even if I am being poured out as a drink offering upon the sacrifice and service of your faith, I rejoice and share my joy with you all.

18   And you too, I urge you, rejoice in the same way and share your joy with me.

Language

a. *Vocabulary:* Define *grumbling; blameless; perverse; word of life; drink offering.*

b. *Style:* List the metaphors and images Paul uses. How do they affect the passage?

Historical

What do we learn of Paul's past relationship with the Philippians?

How does Paul feel about the possibility of his martyrdom?

How should the Philippians feel?

Theological

What are Christians called to do?

What will be the result?

Tactical

How does Paul intend to affect the Philippians in this passage as they face his earlier exhortations?

Contemporary

Judging from these verses why haven't Christians always shone as lights in the world?

Personal

When you are not a light to the people around you do you know the reasons?

Explain them.

INDUCTIVE QUESTIONS FOR PHILIPPIANS 2:19-24

19 But I hope in the Lord Jesus to send Timothy to you shortly, so that I also may be encouraged when I learn of your condition.

20 For I have no one else of kindred spirit who will genuinely be concerned for your welfare.

21 For they all seek after their own interests, not those of Christ Jesus.

22 But you know of his proven worth that he served with me in the furtherance of the gospel like a child serving his father.

23 Therefore I hope to send him immediately, as soon as I see how things go with me;

24 and I trust in the Lord that I myself also shall be coming shortly.

Language

a. *Vocabulary:* Define *kindred spirit; welfare.*

b. *Style:* What kind of information does Paul give in these verses?
   What imagery does he use?

Historical

Describe Paul's relationship with Timothy.
Why was he so anxious to send him to Philippi?

Theological

Was Paul conscious of his influence on Timothy (compare 3:17)?
How did his relationship with Timothy help to spread the gospel?
What can we learn from it for the church today?

Tactical

How would the news of Timothy's coming affect the Philippians in their situation?
How would Timothy's example minister to them?

Contemporary

What is Christian education like around you?

What can be done to create maturing relationships such as Paul and Timothy had?

Personal

Is there a "Paul" in your life?

Is there a "Timothy"? Has there been?

INDUCTIVE QUESTIONS FOR PHILIPPIANS 2:25-30

25   But I thought it necessary to send to you Epaphroditus, my brother and fellow-worker and fellow-soldier, who is also your messenger and minister to my need;

26   because he was longing for you all and was distressed because you had heard that he was sick.

27   For indeed he was sick to the point of death, but God had mercy on him, and not on him only but also on me, lest I should have sorrow upon sorrow.

28   Therefore I have sent him all the more eagerly in order that when you see him again you may rejoice and I may be less concerned about you.

29   Therefore receive him in the Lord with all joy, and hold men like him in high regard;

30   because he came close to death for the work of Christ, risking his life to complete what was deficient in your service to me.

Language

Style: What emphasis does the repetition give in Paul's description of Epaphroditus?

How is the style of this passage related to the style of the preceding one?

Historical

Who was Epaphroditus?
What had he done?
Why was he returning to Philippi?
What was his relationship with Paul like?

Theological

What do Paul's descriptive terms for Epaphroditus reveal about his view of the Christian life, his calling, and fellow-Christians?

What does his relationship with Epaphroditus teach us about godly leadership?

Tactical

What impact will Epaphroditus's return have upon the Philippians?

How will Paul's relationship with Epaphroditus aid the exhortation in 2:1-11?

Contemporary
How does Paul's relationship with other Christians compare with those of the Christian leaders around you?

Would people in the church today risk death for their leaders?

Why or why not?

Personal
How costly is your commitment?

Could someone say about you what Paul said in 2:30?

INDUCTIVE QUESTIONS FOR PHILIPPIANS 3:1
Finally, my brethren, rejoice in the Lord. To write the same things again is no trouble to me, and it is a safeguard for you.

Language
a. *Vocabulary:* Define *safeguard.*

b. *Style:* How does this passage complete the two paragraphs before?
What is the key word that signals the purpose of this verse?

Historical

Is what Paul writes in this letter being said for the first time?
Could this be a method of his teaching?

Theological

Briefly look at the first two chapters and note everything that gives Paul joy. Is he a good example for his call to "rejoice in the Lord"?

Tactical

How will this verse help the Philippians face their problems?

Contemporary

Where are some of the places that people in our society look for joy?

On the whole, is the world around you a joyful place? Why?

Personal

Where do you find your joy?

What does it mean to you to rejoice in the Lord?

INDUCTIVE QUESTIONS FOR PHILIPPIANS 3:2-11

2 *Beware of the dogs, beware of the evil workers, beware of the false circumcision;*

3 *for we are the true circumcision, who worship in the Spirit of God and glory in Christ Jesus and put no confidence in the flesh,*

4 *although I myself might have confidence even in the flesh. If anyone else has a mind to put confidence in the flesh, I far more:*

5 *circumcised the eighth day, of the nation of Israel, of the tribe of Benjamin, a Hebrew of Hebrews, as to the Law, a Pharisee;*

6 *as to zeal, a persecutor of the church; as to the righteousness which is in the Law, found blameless.*

7 *But whatever things were gain to me, those things I have counted as loss for the sake of Christ.*

8 *More than that, I count all things to be loss in view of the surpassing value of knowing Christ Jesus my Lord,*

for whom I have suffered the loss of all things, and count them but rubbish in order that I may gain Christ,

9 *and may be found in Him, not having a righteousness of my own derived from the Law, but that which is through faith in Christ, the righteousness which comes from God on the basis of faith,*

10 *that I may know Him, and the power of His resurrection and the fellowship of His sufferings, being conformed to His death;*

11 *in order that I may attain to the resurrection from among the dead.*

Language

a. *Vocabulary:* Define *the flesh; zeal; faith.*

b. *Style:* Who is emphasized in verses 4-6? In 7-11? What is the significance of the repetition of words and ideas?

Historical

What do you learn about the church's opponents?
How did Paul feel about them?
What do you learn about Paul's own history?

Theological
What were the elements of Paul's religion before he met Christ and what happened to them after his conversion?

What is the focus of his new Christian life?

Tactical
How do these verses help the Philippians deal with their opponents?

Contemporary
Which of the two life-styles prevails among Christians today—justification by faith or justification by works?

Personal
What are you seeking in your Christian life?

INDUCTIVE QUESTIONS FOR PHILIPPIANS 3:12-16
12 Not that I have already obtained it, or have already become perfect, but I press on in order that I may

lay hold of that for which also I was laid hold of by Christ Jesus.

13 Brethren, I do not regard myself as having laid hold of it yet; but one thing I do: forgetting what lies behind and reaching forward to what lies ahead,

14 I press on toward the goal for the prize of the upward call of God in Christ Jesus.

15 Let us therefore, as many as are perfect, have this attitude; and if in anything you have a different attitude, God will reveal that also to you;

16 however, let us keep living by that same standard to which we have attained.

Language:
a. *Vocabulary:* Define *perfect.*

b. *Style:* What words and ideas are repeated?
   What metaphor is used?
   How do these things illustrate the passage?

Historical
   What does Paul assume about some believers at Philippi?

Theological

What does Paul's view about himself tell us about the Christian life?

Toward what is he striving?

Does Paul's striving mean that he has to earn something from God?

Tactical

What is the impact of having this passage follow Paul's testimony in verses 2-11?

How does it keep the Philippians from reaching false conclusions about the Christian life?

Contemporary

What are some of the prizes that people today are striving toward?

What do you see the modern church striving for?

Personal

How do you view yourself?

Are you seeking any "prizes" in your life?

What are they?

INDUCTIVE QUESTIONS FOR PHILIPPIANS 3:17-21

17   Brethren, join in following my example, and observe those who walk according to the pattern you have in us.

18   For many walk, of whom I often told you, and now tell you even weeping, that they are enemies of the cross of Christ,

19   whose end is destruction, whose god is their appetite, and whose glory is in their shame, who set their minds on earthly things.

20   For our citizenship is in heaven, from which also we eagerly wait for a Savior, the Lord Jesus Christ;

21   who will transform the body of our humble state into conformity with the body of His glory, by the exertion of the power that He has even to subject all things to Himself.

Language

a. *Vocabulary:* Define *pattern; the cross of Christ; glory; citizenship.*

b. *Style:* What mood do verses 18,19 provoke?
   What is the mood in 20,21?
   What does the contrast do for Paul's point?

Historical

What are the unbelievers in Philippi like?
Did the Philippians have a choice of life-styles?

Theological

What do we learn about Christians here?
What can they look forward to?
What is the future for unbelievers?

Tactical

What influence would the vivid contrasts of these verses have on the Philippians' life-style?

Contemporary

What kind of alternative life-styles exist today for the Christian?

Do people today live like those described in verse 19?

What is the Christian option?

Personal

What kinds of life-styles tempt you away from Christ?

What do you do about it?

What should you do?

INDUCTIVE QUESTIONS FOR PHILIPPIANS 4:1

Therefore, my beloved brethren whom I long to see, my joy and crown, so stand firm in the Lord, my beloved.

Language

a. *Vocabulary:* Define *crown.*

b. *Style:* What does the "therefore" indicate?

What is the tone of the verse?

Historical
What is said about Paul and the Philippians?

Theological
What is seen about Christian relationships?
In what way are the Philippians Paul's crown?

Tactical
How does Paul's passionate language strengthen his exhortation?
What temptations have caused this verse to be written?

Contemporary
Do Christians today have the same passion for one another as Paul had for the brethren?
Why or why not?
How would a call to "stand firm in the Lord" influence the current state of the church?

Personal
What does it mean to you to stand firm in the Lord?
What false "Christian" footing is there to stand on?

INDUCTIVE QUESTIONS FOR PHILIPPIANS 4:2,3
2   I urge Euodia and I urge Syntyche to live in harmony in the Lord.

3   Indeed, true comrade, I ask you also to help these women who have shared my struggle in the cause of the gospel, together with Clement also, and the rest of my fellow-workers, whose names are in the book of life.

Language
a. *Vocabulary:* Define *comrade; book of life.*

b. *Style:* Does Paul exhort in generalities?

Historical
What do we learn about Euodia and Syntyche?
What had been Paul's relationship with these women?

Theological
What light does this passage shed on the role of women in the church?

Tactical
What does Paul accomplish by admonishing the two women in a public letter?

Contemporary
What does Paul's relationship with these two women have to say to our culture and women and to the church and women?

Personal
Who are the women who have had significant influence on your Christian life?

Do you personally know of any cases of female discrimination?

How do you respond to them?

INDUCTIVE QUESTIONS FOR PHILIPPIANS 4:4-7

4 *Rejoice in the Lord always; again I will say, re-*
joice!

5 *Let your forbearing spirit be known to all men.*
The Lord is near.

6 *Be anxious for nothing, but in everything by*
prayer and supplication with thanksgiving let your re-
quests be made known to God.

7 *And the peace of God, which surpasses all compre-*
hension, shall guard your hearts and your minds in
Christ Jesus.

Language

a. *Vocabulary:* Define *forbearing; supplication.*

b. *Style:* With what kind of attitude does Paul write
   this?

Historical

Theological

Why can a Christian rejoice?

How can a Christian find peace?

Where does that peace come from?

Does God give you peace by changing the circumstances?

Tactical

What do these verses encourage the Philippians to do with their problems of division and opposition?

Contemporary

Anxiety is a modern-day epidemic. What do we commonly use as treatment?

What causes Paul's method of anxiety relief to be overlooked?

Personal

What are some of the things which keep you from claiming the peace of God?

Have you experienced anxiety which has been good for you?

INDUCTIVE QUESTIONS FOR PHILIPPIANS 4:8,9

8 *Finally, brethren, whatever is true, whatever is honorable, whatever is right, whatever is pure, whatever is lovely, whatever is of good repute, if there is any excellence and if anything worthy of praise, let your mind dwell on these things.*

9 *The things you have learned and received and heard and seen in me, practice these things; and the God of peace shall be with you.*

Language
Style: How is Paul communicating?

Historical
What is here about Paul and the Philippians?

Theological
How can a person abide with the God of peace?

In the beginning of verse 9 does Paul mean that he is perfect?

What is he?

If you imitate Paul what will be the result?

Tactical
How does this passage encourage the Philippians to face their problem of disunity?

These verses are meant to focus the Philippians on whom?

Contemporary
Do Christians in the world today offer leadership the same way Paul does in verse 9?

Why? If not, what does the church use to teach Christian living?

What kind of leadership do people need?

Personal

Can you honestly put verse 9 into your vocabulary?
What would keep you from doing so?
What would make you think that you could?

INDUCTIVE QUESTIONS FOR PHILIPPIANS 4:10-13

10   But I rejoiced in the Lord greatly, that now at last you have revived your concern for me; indeed, you were concerned before, but you lacked opportunity.

11   Not that I speak from want; for I have learned to be content in whatever circumstances I am.

12   I know how to get along with humble means, and I also know how to live in prosperity; in any and every circumstance I have learned the secret of being filled and going hungry, both of having abundance and suffering need.

13   I can do all things through Him who strengthens me.

Language
    Vocabulary: Define *content.*

Historical
    What is exposed about the Philippians?
    About Paul?

Theological
    How does Paul relate to circumstances?
    What is the secret of Paul's contentment?
    What do we learn about Christ?

Tactical
    What does Paul specifically do in verse 10?
    Keeping in mind the circumstances the Philippians
are in, what importance do these verses have?

Contemporary
    How do circumstances dictate the welfare of people
around you?

How does material wealth cloud the secret of Paul's contentment?

Personal

Is it easier for you to trust Christ in plenty or in need?

How do your circumstances affect you now?

How does the Lord want you to face your circumstances?

INDUCTIVE QUESTIONS FOR PHILIPPIANS 4:14-20

14   Nevertheless, you have done well to share with me in my affliction.

15   And you yourselves also know, Philippians, that at the first preaching of the gospel, after I departed from Macedonia, no church shared with me in the matter of giving and receiving but you alone;

16   for even in Thessalonica you sent a gift more than once for my needs.

17   Not that I seek the gift itself, but I seek for the profit which increases to your account.

18   But I have received everything in full, and have an abundance; I am amply supplied, having received from Epaphroditus what you have sent, a fragrant aroma, an acceptable sacrifice, well pleasing to God.

19   And my God shall supply all your needs according to His riches in glory in Christ Jesus.

20   Now to our God and Father be the glory forever and ever. Amen.

Language

a. *Vocabulary:* Define *Macedonia; Thessalonica.*

b. *Style:* What is the tone of this passage?

Historical

What have the Philippians done?
How did Paul respond?

Theological

What does Paul consider the Philippians' gift to be?
Although the Philippians gave him money who does Paul say supplies people's needs?
Comment.

Tactical

How does Paul affirm the Philippians' faithful service?

Contemporary

What was one way that the Philippians worshiped God?

How does this differ from today's common view of worship?

Personal

If you firmly believed that God would supply your every need, not out of His riches but according to them, would your life change? How?

INDUCTIVE QUESTIONS FOR PHILIPPIANS 4:21,22

21   Greet every saint in Christ Jesus. The brethren who are with me greet you.

22   All the saints greet you, especially those of Caesar's household.

Language

a. *Vocabulary:* Define *Caesar's household.*

b. *Style:* What does this passage contain?
   What key word is repeated?

Historical
Who was with Paul?
What do we learn of Paul's location?

Theological
Why is there such a free flow of greetings?
What do these people have in common?
What do these verses say about the universality of the church?

Tactical
What purpose do the farewells serve?
Why does Paul mention those who are with him?

Contemporary
Paul emphasized the unique identity and the family bond of Christians.

Are these qualities needed in today's world?

Where do people seek them outside of Christ?

Personal
What things can stand between you and a fellow-believer in Christ?

INDUCTIVE QUESTIONS FOR PHILIPPIANS 4:23
23 *The grace of the Lord Jesus Christ be with your spirit.*

Language
Style: What is this type of verse traditionally called?

Historical

Theological

What does it mean for the grace of Christ to be with a Christian's spirit?

Tactical

Why does Paul end his letter calling on the grace of Christ?

Contemporary

Only the grace of the Lord Jesus can bring peace to a soul.

What things can you point to in our world that are signs that souls are restless without Christ?

Personal

What would it mean for you to leave someone by commending the grace of Christ to be with his spirit?

Part II

Commentary on Philippians

INDUCTIVE QUESTIONS FOR PHILIPPIANS 1:1

Paul and Timothy, bond-servants of Christ Jesus, to all the saints in Christ Jesus who are in Philippi, including the overseers and deacons:

Language

a. *Vocabulary: bond-servants*—literally "slave"; Paul and Timothy are in bondage to Christ; *saints*—those set apart from the world by accepting Christ, "Christians"; *Philippi*—a city in Macedonia, northern Greece; *deacons*—literally "waiters," those who serve, see Acts 6:1-6.

b. *Style:* A salutation form of address: "Paul ... to the saints." Here the author and the recipients are mentioned.

Historical

Paul is with Timothy as he writes this letter. Timothy shares his identity and authority. The Apostle designates them both as servants or slaves belonging to

Christ. Timothy is apparently known to the church.

All the Christians in Philippi are addressed in this letter. The church is an organized body with "overseers and deacons." The overseers supervise the spiritual life of the congregation, and the deacons minister.

Theological

Paul identifies himself and Timothy as "bond-servants of Christ Jesus." The Apostle can proclaim himself free in Christ and yet a servant of Christ. How is this possible? For Paul the answer is that Christ has made him for Himself. It is in surrender to Christ that Paul discovers why he is created, and thus his true freedom.

A servant has position depending upon whom he serves. Paul serves the King—this is his destiny and dignity.

All Christians are "saints," not because of what they do in living a holy life, but because of what Christ has done in setting them free from the world. They live both "in Philippi" and "in Christ." While free from the world we must live in it as preserving salt and illumining light (see Matt. 5:13,14). We prefer to be only "in Christ," but Christ prefers us also to be "in Philippi."

The church is structured with "overseers" and "deacons." We are called to total responsibility for each other in a caring community. This must be lived out in the life of the church.

Tactical

Paul introduces both himself and Timothy as "bond-servants." In other letters he often appeals to his apostolic authority, but not here. Why not? One reason is that because of the Philippians' love, the Apostle need not flash his credentials to impress them. Another is that in exhorting them to humility as the ground for unity (2:1-11) he must model this attitude himself.

Notice also the word "all." Paul refuses to take sides in a divided church. He will speak to "all" as he calls them to the "attitude of Christ" (2:5).

Contemporary

It is popular today to call for a spontaneous Christian life and a spontaneous church. We rightly are suspicious of ritual and organization. Forms become empty; power corrupts. Paul, however, addresses "overseers and deacons." The church at Philippi had its officers. Someone was responsible.

Freedom without form becomes chaos. The answer to a dead church is not to disorganize, rather, it is to call the organization to its biblical foundations and to a recovery of the reasons God had in establishing it. Overseers and deacons were given to promote the whole ministry of the Christian body. We have the same needs today. Someone must oversee our spiritual growth. Someone must organize for physical emergency and need. We must call the overseers and deacons not to be corporate boards of directors but to be caring, ministering believers who, accepting responsibility, invest their lives for God's people.

Personal

In reaction to the power structures of the church with its vested interests, I have tended to reject the rightful place of "overseers and deacons" in my life. This, however, is shortsighted.

There are no perfect forms of church life because there are no perfect people. Nevertheless, I need overseers and deacons who accept responsibility for my life.

When I was in college, Donn Moomaw, the All-American football player from UCLA who met Christ through Campus Crusade, came to Princeton Seminary. He began a prayer fellowship on the university campus nearby, and I was invited. Periodically, Donn would come to me and say, "How's your walk with the Lord?" Donn could get away with this because he cared. How I appreciated his accepting responsibility for my life; he was my overseer. I continue to need such today.

INDUCTIVE QUESTIONS FOR PHILIPPIANS 1:2

2 *Grace to you and peace from God our Father and the Lord Jesus Christ.*

Language
a. *Vocabulary: grace*—God's free, undeserved forgiveness and acceptance; *peace*—wholeness; *Father*—the source of all, a term of intimacy; *Lord*—sovereign, the Greek translation of the Old Testament name for God.
b. *Style:* A standard blessing.

Historical

Theological
We can never hear enough of the gospel. We are such sinners, our hearts are so hard, we are in constant need of "grace and peace." "Grace," acceptance, yields "peace," wholeness. All comes from "God our Father" and "the Lord Jesus Christ."

Notice that God is "our" Father. He belongs to us and we to Him. The unknowable, holy, utterly transcendent God has become knowable—and not as judge, but Father.

Notice also that Jesus is "the" Lord, not one among many. He shares no sovereignty. As the old saying has it, He is either "Lord of all" or not Lord "at all."

Tactical

Contemporary

What do the church and the world need? The answers are many: security, wealth, power, freedom—so the words are multiplied.

What does Paul offer? The standard blessing—"grace and peace." We can never get beyond our need of the gospel. We assume that we know what we need. God alone, however, really knows and His offer is "grace and peace," acceptance and wholeness. Apart from His salvation gift there is nothing but darkness and night. The politicians promise, business leaders plan, psychologists analyze, professors critique; only God offers and gives grace and peace.

Personal

How often I settle for less than the final, real solution. How often I am a sucker for half-truths. Advertisers offer me happiness with a new car, freedom with an insurance policy, fulfillment in a vacation trip. But I purchase and consume only to be left dissatisfied. Now God comes—here is "grace and peace." "I am the source and the means, look nowhere else," He claims. Often as a last resort rather than as a first response I come back. "Thou hast made us for thyself and our hearts are restless until they rest in Thee" (Augustine).

INDUCTIVE QUESTIONS FOR PHILIPPIANS 1:3-11

3 *I thank my God in all my remembrance of you,*

4 *always offering prayer with joy in my every prayer for you all,*

5 *in view of your participation in the gospel from the first day until now.*

6 *For I am confident of this very thing, that He who began a good work in you will perfect it until the day of Christ Jesus.*

7 *For it is only right for me to feel this way about you*

all, because I have you in my heart, since both in my imprisonment and in the defense and confirmation of the gospel, you all are partakers of grace with me.

8   For God is my witness, how I long for you all with the affection of Christ Jesus.

9   And this I pray, that your love may abound still more and more in real knowledge and all discernment,

10   so that you may approve the things that are excellent, in order to be sincere and blameless until the day of Christ;

11   having been filled with the fruit of righteousness which comes through Jesus Christ, to the glory and praise of God.

Language

a. *Vocabulary: joy*—gladness, happiness, a sense of exhilaration; *gospel*—good news, God's gladness; *the day of Jesus Christ*—the second coming of Christ in power and glory at the end of this age. *Grace*—see 1:2; *love*—self-giving care without regard for the value of the object; *discernment*—discrimination; *sincere*—one quality without any foreign substance; *blameless*—no moral deviation; *righteousness*—right-standing before God, a legal term, "not guilty"; *glory*—"brightness," that which brings praise to God.

b. *Style:* The form is liturgical, that of a prayer. It is broken into two sections: thanksgiving—"I thank my God" (1:3); and intercession—"And this I pray, that . . ." (1:9). Notice the use of "all" six times.

Historical

Paul thanks God for the Philippians' "participation in the gospel from the first day until now" (1:5). This participation includes their financial support of his ministry (4:14-18). The "first day" is the day of their conversion.

The "now" is up to the present moment. Thus, the Philippians have supported Paul throughout their acquaintance with him.

Moreover, by their gifts of money and the sending of Epaphroditus (2:25-30), they are partaking in grace in the Apostle's imprisonment as he defends and confirms the gospel (1:7). Rather than their financial support being a burden, it is a sharing in the grace of God as they share Paul's ministry.

Now Paul yearns for the Philippians. He is free to express deep emotional feelings for them, being bound to them in the "affection of Christ Jesus" (1:8).

Theological

The Apostle expresses his thanksgiving to God for the Philippians. He attributes their support and encouragement of him, however, to grace. Their good works (1:5) are a result of God's good work. "For I am confident of this very thing, that He who began a good work in you will perfect it until the day of Christ Jesus" (1:6). Christian service is to bring glory not to ourselves, but to our "Father who is in heaven" (Matt. 5:16). This is its true test: do I see the hand of God in what I do? Does it point beyond me to Christ?

In his confidence that God will complete the good work he has begun, Paul expresses essential trust in the faithfulness, power and perfection of God. God does not leave His work half-finished. Furthermore, on the day of Jesus Christ it will be complete. History ends at the feet of Christ. Regardless of the present inconsistencies and contradictions in our human experience, the goal is certain. All will be perfected when Christ comes for us.

As the Apostle prays for the Philippians (1:9-11), so he expresses the essential elements of Christian character.

The primary element is love, "And this I pray, that

your love may abound still more and more" (1:9). Paul desires love to become both more intensive and extensive in the life of his converts. Without love, all else is sham (see 1 Cor. 13:1-3).

This love is the very self-giving, sacrificial love of Christ which is extravagant and uncalculating. It is not, however, sentimental and mindless. Therefore, Paul prays that it be tempered with "knowledge and all discernment." We are to love with Christ's love and this means to love in truth. "Speaking the truth in love, we are to grow up in all aspects into Him, who is the head, even Christ" (Eph. 4:15). Love without knowledge has no depth. It easily becomes mere emotion, changing like the wind.

As we love in truth, with content, with knowledge, the Apostle also prays for "discernment." Knowledge is to become valuable and functional as it gives us the basis for testing the spirits (see 1 John 4:1). We are to discern who the true Christians are. We are to discern proper motives for witness and service. We are to discern moral issues and conflicts. All of this will then have a proper result: "So that you may approve the things that are excellent, in order to be sincere and blameless until the day of Christ" (Phil. 1:10). Love, knowledge and discernment have a moral direction; we are being conformed to Christ as we grow and await His return.

Now we will approve the excellent, not settling for even the good when we can have the best. Our inner holiness or "wholeness" will be accomplished by the love in truth operating in our lives. Notice that practical holiness is the result not the presupposition of love and truth. As our hearts are filled with Christ's love and our minds are dominated by His truth, a fragrant life of integrity will emerge. Paul is then confident that we will be "filled with the fruit of righteousness which comes through Jesus Christ, to the glory and praise of God"

(1:11). Having the root of righteousness from Christ, we will bear the fruit of righteousness through Christ. This fruit includes the whole scope of Christian character (see Gal. 5:22,23). Notice again that, as in our good works (Phil. 1:5,6), so in our moral character (1:10,11), we can take no credit. The glory and praise go to God. It is His work. For this we are both grateful and relieved. Thus, Paul prays. For God to do this we are to relax and let Him accomplish His own work in us.

Tactical

Paul addresses a giving church with appropriate thanksgiving for their participation in the gospel (1:5). This has been expressed again and again by monetary gifts (2:25-30; 4:14-18).

Paul also addresses a suffering church (1:29,30). Thus he is confident that although they may go through the fire and even experience martyrdom, God will complete His good work (1:6).

Furthermore, Paul addresses a church troubled by legalists who demand good works for salvation (3:2ff.). Against this he promises that God will complete His own good work. The Philippians must not rely upon their human effort to prepare for Christ's day (1:6). Also, as they grow in love and truth they will grow in holiness and its fruit which come not from moral effort but "through Jesus Christ." The glory goes not to the Philippians, but to God (1:11).

Finally, Paul addresses a divided church. Notice the stress on "all" (1:3,4,7,8). The Apostle refuses to take sides. His love goes to *all* who believe. At the same time, he prays for an increase in their love, so that the wounds may be healed without theological or moral compromise (1:9).

Thus we see how Paul's introductory prayer is related to the specific needs of the Philippians. Understanding those needs helps us to see how the Apostle's prayer anticipates the rest of his letter. We also see how concretely he intercedes for his converts.

Contemporary

Paul sees the future dominated by the day of Jesus Christ (1:6,10). Life in this world is a preparation for that day.

The world, of course, has no consciousness of this. Chemist Sir George Porter, for example, writes in the *Los Angeles Times* (Feb. 6, 1975) that the function of science must now be to meet the spiritual needs of men, because the old religions are outdated. Having solved our physical problems, scientists must find "a new faith, a new purpose in life." This will come for Sir George through "physics, chemistry, biology," as man is studied by these disciplines. Questions must be pursued such as "what is it that we want man to achieve?" As we discover a better understanding of man, "our ethics and morals must ultimately be derived from this better understanding." Sir George asks, "What may we not achieve in the four billion years which remain before the earth becomes uninhabitable?"

What vision of the future is given here? For Sir George man can solve his own problems. Science holds the key to all questions. The study of man will answer religious needs. We can find our meaning working for generations yet to come. All will ultimately end in four billion years with an uninhabitable earth.

Sir George offers a strange mixture of humanistic optimism and final doom.

Over against this man-centered philosophy stands biblical faith. Our destiny is fulfilled not in some future generation, our destiny is fulfilled in Jesus Christ. His gospel is the solution which we bear to the world now. History will end not with the cooling of the planet but with the coming of Christ. Not a silent void but a reigning person stands as the goal of all creation, time and life. We are thus responsible to Him for we shall stand before Him.

This hope must be renewed in the church and proclaimed in the world. We look not even just to the salvation of our own souls and heavenly bliss. We look for the triumph of the day of Christ. May we long for and live for that day!

Personal

Philippians is filled with intensely emotional language: "offering prayer with joy, I have you in my heart"; "I long for you all with the affection of Christ Jesus." Paul is unafraid to bind his church to himself with the ties of love. How do I feel about expressing such feelings to Christians about me?

My first problem is cultural: men do not express their emotions. This is for "weak women." But is this so? Jesus wept at Lazarus' tomb. Jesus was the only perfect man. Am I free then to cry?

My second problem is personal: if I let my feelings out, will they be accepted? Not necessarily. This is the risk I must take. How will people know they are loved by God if I am unable to make them feel loved by me? The Word must become flesh in my flesh. Here is the incarnate gospel.

My "natural reserve," my male stereotypes, my fears of rejection must all be abandoned for the sake of Christ. May I be as vulnerable and warm as Paul was to the Philippians, affirming and thanking people, letting them know that for Christ's sake they are loved and they are loved by *me*!

INDUCTIVE QUESTIONS FOR PHILIPPIANS 1:12-14

12 *Now I want you to know, brethren, that my cir-*

cumstances have turned out for the greater progress of the gospel,

13 so that my imprisonment in the cause of Christ has become well-known throughout the whole praetorian guard and to everyone else,

14 and that most of the brethren, trusting in the Lord because of my imprisonment, have far more courage to speak the word of God without fear.

Language

a. *Vocabulary: praetorian guard*—the elite Roman army guard assigned to the emperor and used in guarding state prisoners; *brethren*—a family metaphor for Christians.

b. *Style:* Paul now turns to the body of the letter. "Now I want you to know, brethren . . ." (1:12). Compare Galatians 1:11, "For I would have you know, brethren . . ." and 2 Corinthians 1:8, "For we do not want you to be unaware, brethren . . ."

Historical

Paul is in prison, probably in Rome. He has had opportunity in this confinement to share his faith with the soldiers guarding him and "to everyone else," probably meaning slaves working in the prison and other inmates (1:13). The example of his boldness has encouraged the Christians on the outside to be likewise bold in their witness (1:14).

Theological

Evangelism is not just "presence," it is "proclamation." Paul does not just offer a Christian example in prison, he offers the gospel. The result of this is knowledge (1:13), all know the *substance* of his imprisonment as being "for Christ."

For those on the outside, this bold proclamation

breeds confidence "to speak the word of God without fear" (1:14). Again, other Christians are not merely willing to accept suffering because of Paul's example. They are willing to preach. Biblical evangelism proceeds where proclamation is at its heart. It is only in the speaking of the good news that truth will be heard and Christian example and motivation become clear. This announcement of Christ is the "word of God," not the mere opinion of men. God yet speaks through His servants.

Tactical

The Philippians are facing persecution (1:29,30). Paul shares his imprisonment with them not merely to update them with personal news, but to prepare them to share his destiny.

The question is, how do you equip people to suffer for Christ? Part of the answer is by good theology; part of the answer is by prayer and the Holy Spirit; but part of the answer is also by the example of other Christians who have already gone through it.

Thus Paul shows here how adverse circumstances have turned out as an advantage for the gospel. What must have been a source of great discouragement of the church, namely the Apostle's incarceration, has really opened up a new mission field—prison evangelism. Paul has become chaplain to the praetorian guard.

This boldness has also encouraged boldness by those on the outside (1:14). Thus the gospel advances within and without.

So if the Philippians are to be arrested for their witness, they must trust Christ and profit from Paul's experience. They are not to be prisoners of adverse circumstances. If their identity is in Christ, if their calling in this world is to witness to Christ, a prison or hospital bed may be a better pulpit than that of any church.

Contemporary

Most people today are victims of their environment. They are constantly reacting rather than acting. If we view our problems as circumstantial, then we look for circumstantial answers—a change in job, a vacation, a new living arrangement, cheaper gasoline. Christians must care about the environment. A change may be good. It is crass and heartless to propose the saving of souls without caring for physical and social needs.

It is, however, just as crass to propose that a new environment, a new set of circumstances, is *the* answer. We may move to Hawaii "to get away from it all." But we discover, to our dismay, that in the move we cannot escape ourselves. We are our biggest problem.

Many times the circumstances cannot be changed. But we can be changed—our vision, our attitudes, our motives, our goals. Paul could not escape prison but he could escape discouragement and frustration. His secret? Viewing prison as an opportunity for Christ. Since Paul's imprisonment was "in the cause of Christ" (1:13), the Apostle was certain that Christ wanted him there, and thus was there with him to use this adversity for His own purpose and glory. It is either circumstances or the lordship of Christ. One or the other will determine our lives. We must make the choice.

Personal

The gospel secret is that God brings life out of death. In our weakness, the strength of Christ is seen (see 2 Cor. 12:1-10). For Paul, glory comes out of prison. Guards and other prisoners will inherit eternity because of the Apostle's lockup.

When I was growing up I was frustrated by two problems. I had little mechanical skills and I was too light to play sports. Furthermore, I was subject to a nervous condition which affected my heart and made heavy exercise difficult. Since my high school world was dominated by athletes, I was embarrassed and frustrated because I could not compete. For these reasons my energies went into studies and public speaking. When I came to know Christ, He took these energies and talents and used them for His own purposes. I have often thought in retrospect how grateful I should be that I could not devote hours daily to the athletic field. It was a frustration at the time, but in the grace of God this adversity opened the doors to a major university scholarship and later graduate school.

Again and again I must relearn an old truth. God works in what I view as adversity to accomplish His purpose for His glory. Can I say with Paul "my imprisonment [is] in the cause of Christ"? Help me, Lord, to be so trusting.

INDUCTIVE QUESTIONS FOR PHILIPPIANS 1:15-18

15 *Some, to be sure, are preaching Christ even from envy and strife, but some also from good will;*

16 *the latter do it out of love, knowing that I am appointed for the defense of the gospel;*

17 *the former proclaim Christ out of selfish ambition, rather than from pure motives, thinking to cause me distress in my imprisonment.*

18 *What then? Only that in every way, whether in pretense or in truth, Christ is proclaimed; and in this I rejoice, yes, and I will rejoice.*

Language

a. *Vocabulary: rejoice*—a sense of gladness over the fulfillment of one's conviction or purpose.

b. *Style:* The paragraph is structured by two groups: "some ... some" (1:15); "the latter ... the former" (1:16,17). "What then?" (1:18) introduces Paul's conclusion in a rhetorical style.

Historical

While Paul is in prison there are two groups on the outside engaging in evangelism. The first preaches Christ out of proper motives, "good will" (1:15), "out of love" (1:16). The second preaches out of improper motives, "from envy and strife" (1:15), "out of selfish ambition, rather than from pure motives, thinking to cause me distress in my imprisonment" (1:17).

This elaboration of the responses to Paul's imprisonment shows that the Apostle continues to provoke division wherever he goes. The stormy opposition to him from the legalistic Hebrew Christians and their followers dealt with in Galatians, and the "superlative Apostle" who invaded the Corinthian church (see 2 Cor. 10—13) illustrate this. Now in Rome, Christians are again divided by the Apostle. Those who oppose him have seized upon his imprisonment as their opportunity to gain converts to their side. Others, however, respond from genuine motives seeking to fill the gap left by Paul's absence.

Theological

Paul demonstrates a generous spirit here in refusing to judge or reject those who preach Christ from impure motives. This is in sharp contrast to Galatians where he denounces those who pervert the gospel (see Gal. 1:6ff.). Why the change?

The decisive difference is that now only the motives are wrong, not the message. As long as Christ is proclaimed, Paul's passion and purpose are accomplished (1:18). God will be the determiner of motives. If, however, the gospel itself is tainted, the Apostle will rise to the occasion. This we shall see in Philippians itself: "Beware of the dogs, beware of the evil workers, beware of the false circumcision" (3:2). The Christian is to let God be the judge of motives. We are to judge results.

100

"You will know them by their fruits" (Matt. 7:20).

Tactical

Paul continues to elaborate upon the progress of the gospel in light of his imprisonment. Even though evangelistic motives are mixed, the results prove again that God is the Lord of adversity, using it to advance His purpose.

Contemporary

How are we to respond to those who preach Christ from base motives? The answer from Paul is one word: generosity. When we suspect that a person shares Christ improperly this does not mean silence. We are responsible to exhort and rebuke the brethren. Our exhortation, however, may be wrong. God alone knows our hearts (see 1 Sam. 16:7). We cannot finally say that even our own motives are pure. Thus we live by the forgiveness of our sins.

Does Pastor X seem to be on an ego-trip? Does Pastor Y justify his ministry with big budget, plant and membership? These are not the questions which determine our fellowship. The only relevant question is, do they preach Christ?

"Counterculture" Christians are often critical of Campus Crusade for Christ for packaging evangelistic tools after the pattern of American salesmanship. "Crusaders" may challenge Young Life for soft-selling the gospel by investing too much time in building relationships. Inter-Varsity followers often judge other evangelistic efforts for lack of intellectual depth. The church questions all of these groups for not carrying on evangelism within its walls and programs. So it goes. What does Paul say from prison? Forget methods. Forget motives. "Only that in every way, whether in pretense or in truth, Christ is proclaimed; and in this I rejoice."

Personal

I have learned that Christ meets people through many different means.

Since I met Christ through Young Life, my preference tends toward relational evangelism. This also best fits my personality structure. Many come to Christ, however, in other ways. Donn Moomaw, ex-UCLA All-American football player and now pastor of Bel Air Presbyterian Church, prayed to receive Christ in the living room of Bill Bright, founder of Campus Crusade for Christ. My own cousin, Dave Walker, became a Christian in his fraternity after a Campus Crusade team came there. He now serves Christ as a Methodist pastor. Rob Langworthy, who has just received his Ph.D. in philosophy from Yale, accepted Christ after reading a Campus Crusade *Four Spiritual Laws* booklet while he was an undergraduate at Claremont Men's College. Yes, "Christ is proclaimed; and in this I rejoice."

INDUCTIVE QUESTIONS FOR PHILIPPIANS 1:19-26

19 For I know that this shall turn out for my deliverance through your prayers and the provision of the Spirit of Jesus Christ,

20 according to my earnest expectation and hope, that I shall not be put to shame in anything, but that with all boldness, Christ shall even now, as always, be exalted in my body, whether by life or by death.

21 For to me, to live is Christ, and to die is gain.

22 But if I am to live on in the flesh, this will mean fruitful labor for me; and I do not know which to choose.

23 But I am hard pressed from both directions, having the desire to depart and be with Christ, for that is very much better;

24 yet to remain on in the flesh is more necessary for your sake.

25 And convinced of this, I know that I shall remain

*and continue with you all for your progress and joy in
the faith,*

26   *so that your proud confidence in me may abound
in Christ Jesus through my coming to you again.*

Language

a. *Vocabulary: the Spirit of Jesus Christ*—the Holy
Spirit, the third person of the Trinity, God's immi-
nent presence with us; *the flesh*—present, historical
existence, here, morally neutral in contrast to its
meaning in Philippians 3:3; *the faith*—the substance
of the gospel and life.

b. *Style:* Paul's style is intensely personal here; notice
his use of "I." At the same time, Christ's name appears five times. Thus the vocabulary shows us how
Christ-centered the Apostle's life is. The basic contrast here is between life and death.

Historical

Paul stands between two desires. The first is to go and
be with Christ (1:23); the second is to remain in this
world serving the Philippians (1:24-26). Because of their
needs, he trusts that he will join them again (1:19).

Meanwhile, they are to pray for his deliverance (1:19)
so that when he returns to them, their "proud confidence . . . may abound in Christ Jesus" (1:26).

Theological

Paul deals with two fundamental issues here in the
light of Jesus Christ. We may pose them as questions:
What does it mean to die? What does it mean to live?

Paul replies by first answering a third question: What
is the meaning of Jesus Christ? Hear his response: "According to my earnest expectation and hope, that . . .
Christ shall even now, as always, be exalted in my body,
whether by life or by death" (1:20).

For the Apostle, the service of Jesus Christ, the honor of Jesus Christ, has given life and death their meaning. Paul desires that he will not be ashamed of Christ. He longs for the courage to honor Him "in his body." Christ has liberated Paul from selfishness, having become the focus, center, motivation and goal of his life. Having answered the question of Christ, the questions of life and death are now answered through Him.

Death becomes gain (1:21). In the paraphrase of J.B. Phillips, "to die is to gain more of Christ." Death means departing and being with Christ and this is "very much better" (1:23). The quality of life in Christ which Paul has received cannot be destroyed by death. Christ is the resurrected Lord. He promises that those who believe in Him will "never die" (see John 11:26). We no longer face death alone. Christ has gone through it *for* us. He will go through it *with* us. Nothing, not even death, can separate us from His love (see Rom. 8:38,39).

To depart and be with Christ is "very much better" because it will turn faith to sight (see 1 Cor. 13:12). Paul longs to see the Lord and be fulfilled in His presence. Heaven is also "very much better" because it means the end of sin, suffering, loneliness, anxiety, and death. Furthermore, it means reunion with those who have gone before us in Christ. No wonder Paul longs to depart. Christ gives us an authentic "homesickness" for heaven, to hold His gaze, to be held in His hand, to know and be known. Because we know where we are going, the journey in this world gains authentic meaning.

Life becomes full. Life is Christ (Phil. 1:21), and life is Christians (1:22,24-26). Freed from the fear of death, Paul is able to live with abandonment, "careless" about the future, investing himself in the cause of Christ, which centers in people. His "fruitful labor" is the "progress and joy in the faith" of the Christians at Philippi (1:25). As the Philippians grow in Christ their joy increases. Paul's ministry helps accomplish these results.

Philippians 1:21 is Paul's motto: "For to me, to live is Christ, and to die is gain." It is Christ who, resolving the issues of life and death, gathers the fragments of Paul's life into a whole. Christ places the mark of eternity upon all the Apostle does. He brings unity, purpose, and direction. He is Lord over the life Paul lives. Here is Paul's journey into joy—nothing more or less than Christ.

Tactical

Paul instructs the Philippians in suffering by showing them how the issue of death has been resolved for him. Death is now revalued as "gain" because death is the door into Christ's presence.

At the same time, we will be in this world as long as Christ wills us to be. Where there is "fruitful labor," Christ will keep us here.

Thus while Paul shows his triumph over circumstances in 1:12-18, he shows his triumph over himself in 1:19-26. This is the true triumph which will prepare the Philippians for death or for life.

Contemporary

How does the world face death? By avoidance, by sentimentality, by cynicism, by resignation. The world faces death admitting that death is the final victor. Death is the NO that denies all ultimate meaning to life. Death makes human accomplishment foolish. Death finally consumes all we have done and all that we are. In the words of the hymn, "O God, Our Help in Ages Past":

> Time, like an ever-rolling stream,
> Bears all its sons away,
> They fly, forgotten, as the dream
> Dies at opening day.

But into a world cursed by finitude and transitoriness, Christ has come. The great reversal has been accomplished. Death is swallowed up in life.

I attended a Buddhist sect meeting recently where I was told to chant for my heart's desire and it would be granted. During the question and answer time I inquired as to what these chanters would have to say to a terminal cancer patient. In other words, what was their answer to death?

My question was avoided, but I pressed it. The speaker responded, "We are interested in happiness now, and besides, no one has come back from the dead to tell us anything." I responded, "You are wrong. One person has come back: Jesus Christ."

This is our message to a world under the NO of death. Jesus Christ has come back. Beyond the NO is God's YES. Now to die is gain.

Personal

I had a moving experience last month as Earl and Elizabeth Williamson told me about their son Dennis who died at the age of 23. Dennis had been a Christian for only six months when he was told he had terminal cancer. He now had three years to live.

His life grew through the ups and downs of those years as Dennis gained increasing boldness about his faith. He said, "Cancer brought me to my knees, I had no control over my life."

In an interview at U.C.L.A. Medical Center, Dennis responded to a doctor's question about life by asking him, "Do you want to live a short time for God or a long time for nothing?"

Finally, Dennis was brought home to die. His mother would come into his room and ask her sedated son, "Dennis, are you here?" His reply each time was, "Yes, Mother, I'm here." Near the end she came again with her question. Dennis's reply was, "No, Mother, I'm going home." Dennis, looking about him, cried, "Faith is a lighted room."

A plaque stands over the bed where Dennis died. It reads:

> I hear you Christian
> Riotous, joyful, unafraid.
> Because you know a song
> From the other side of death.

Dennis's mother said to me, "He prepared us to die."

So Dennis has helped me too. As I face the dread of death, possible suffering, the denial of life, loneliness, the unknown, I hear from Dennis songs from the other side. He, like Paul, has found the gain in death. By God's grace may I find it too.

INDUCTIVE QUESTIONS FOR PHILIPPIANS 1:27-30

27 *Only conduct yourselves in a manner worthy of the gospel of Christ; so that whether I come and see you or remain absent, I may hear of you that you are standing firm in one spirit, with one mind striving together for the faith of the gospel;*

28 *in no way alarmed by your opponents—which is a sign of destruction for them, but of salvation for you, and that too, from God.*

29 *For to you it has been granted for Christ's sake, not only to believe in Him, but also to suffer for His sake,*

30 *experiencing the same conflict which you saw in me, and now hear to be in me.*

Language

a. *Vocabulary: salvation*—here, deliverance from an enemy; ultimately, fulfilled in union with God; *granted*—something given by the grace of God.

b. *Style:* Notice the repetition for emphasis: "one spirit," "one mind," "striving together." Notice too the military imagery in 1:27,28; Christians are engaged in spiritual warfare.

Historical

The Philippians have opponents (1:28) who will bring suffering upon them (1:29). This is a continuation of the conflict which they saw in Paul's persecution when he came to evangelize Philippi (1:30), and which they now hear about as he has been imprisoned.

Thus the church, like Paul, is faced with pressure from the Roman authorities who view loyalty to Christ as competition with the claims of the emperor, the state gods and their religious cults.

Theological

A life of unity is a life "worthy of the gospel" (1:27). Why is this? The answer lies in the nature of our message: in Christ God has reconciled the world. If Christians are divided how will non-Christians believe our message? As we stand together we demonstrate the truth we proclaim. Our unity is also a sign that all opposition to God's will, all divisiveness, is doomed to destruction (1:28).

A life of unity is not a life of peace in this world: "For to you it has been granted for Christ's sake, not only to believe in Him, but also suffer for His sake" (1:29).

Paul uses a word here which comes from "grace." "It has been granted" means "this is the grace of God." God's grace is seen not only in our faith but also in our suffering. Where we are attacked for our faith, where we are persecuted, rejected and mocked, this too is a sign of God's grace. Why is this so?

In part, this is true because God counts us worthy to suffer for Christ (see Acts 5:41). He trusts us to take it. It is also true because suffering means we are standing boldly for Christ, not compromising our witness. Furthermore, it is true because God uses our suffering for His glory. Out of the sufferings of Christ He redeemed the world. Out of Paul's sufferings He advanced the gospel. This leads to the deepest truth—out of death comes life. Our God is Lord of suffering. The cross is the sign of our life in this world. In the crucible, God works, as suffering tests our faith, shows it genuine, and stops the mouths of those who mock the gospel.

Tactical

Here Paul shows his deepest intention in 1:12-30; the church, like himself, is facing persecution (1:30). He has prepared the Philippians by his example, and now he also calls them to unity (1:27,28). If they are divided within they will not stand against the pressures from without. Thus, the call to unity in this paragraph becomes a practical bridge to the theology of unity in 2:1-11 in light of a divided church.

Contemporary

Suffering is not popular in the church today. We want to be the church glorified or the church militant but we flee from being the church suffering (Luther).

Certainly this is a sign of our selfishness and defensiveness. But more than this, it is our sign of compromise and capitulation to the world. We want a good-time gospel because we want a good-time life. But as Luther says, this has nothing to do with theology in depth. It also has nothing to do with life in depth.

While we protect ourselves with popular, successful religion, the world suffers and people live lives of "quiet desperation."

Christ calls us to participate in the sufferings of the world. And as we do, paradoxically, we will suffer from the world. We will be misunderstood. We will be unwanted. As we live openly for Christ, caring for people, many of those people will want neither the love nor the truth we bring.

As we are challenged for our faith, however, we become a challenge. Out of our suffering, our faith will shine, and for some this will be a call to life rather than an omen of destruction.

When the church suffers, her real enemies begin to be seen and her real life begins to be lived.

Helmut Thielicke writes that when the bombs destroyed Germany's churches in World War II and scattered the congregations, disrupting their programs, then the Christians learned what they really had, what their life was. What they had was the gospel. Their life was Christ. All else was dispensable. Nothing else mattered. May God not have to rain bombs upon us to teach us the same truth.

Personal

I instinctively flee suffering. Throughout my years as a pastor I easily avoided most of my suffering for Christ by hiding in the church. It is in the world that we will have tribulation (see John 16:33). Then I became a lecturer in religion on a secular college campus. Some students were threatened because of my open stand for Christ. I was accused of evangelizing in the classroom, being anti-Semitic, teaching without intellectual substance. Other religion professors resented me and plotted my removal. Suddenly, in confrontation with the world, verses such as Philippians 1:29 began to live. As for Paul on Mars' Hill, some believed (see Acts 17:32-34), but others did not. I began to see how my commitment to Christ threatened the assumptions and values of secular education. I discovered how ideological and dogmatic so-called "liberalism" had become. I realized that the opposition to me honored me. Here in my life was a sign that God's grace was at work. If my faith led

110

to suffering, I had glad company in Paul, the Philippians and the Lord Jesus Christ.

INDUCTIVE QUESTIONS FOR PHILIPPIANS 2:1-11

1   *If therefore there is any encouragement in Christ, if there is any consolation of love, if there is any fellowship of the Spirit, if any affection and compassion,*

2   *make my joy complete by being of the same mind, maintaining the same love, united in spirit, intent on one purpose.*

3   *Do nothing from selfishness or empty conceit, but with humility of mind let each of you regard one another as more important than himself;*

4   *do not merely look out for your own personal interests, but also for the interests of others.*

5   *Have this attitude in yourselves which was also in Christ Jesus,*

6   *who, although He existed in the form of God, did not regard equality with God a thing to be grasped,*

7   *but emptied Himself, taking the form of a bond-servant, and being made in the likeness of men.*

8   *And being found in appearance as a man, He humbled Himself by becoming obedient to the point of death, even death on a cross.*

9   *Therefore also God highly exalted Him, and bestowed on Him the name which is above every name,*

10   *that at the name of Jesus every knee should bow, of those who are in heaven, and on earth, and under the earth,*

11   *and that every tongue should confess that Jesus Christ is Lord, to the glory of God the Father.*

Language

a. *Vocabulary: the Spirit*—the Holy Spirit see 1:19; *affection*— strong feelings of endearment; *compassion* —positive identification and care for another; *joy*

—see 1:4; *mind*—attitude; *conceit*—pride, falsely valuing oneself above others; *humility*—proper self-evaluation in lowliness after the example of Christ (2:5-8); *form*—that which gives shape to the essence of something; *bond-servant*—slave; *cross*—the agent of executing noncitizen Roman criminals; *exalted*—lifted up to glory; *under the earth*—the lowest parts of the earth, all below mankind; *Lord*—see 1:2; *Father*—see 1:2.

b. *Style:* Paul uses conditional sentences which imply a positive affirmation: "If therefore there is any encouragement ..." meaning, "Since there is encouragement."

Notice the repetition for emphasis as in 1:27: "Same mind," "same love," "one purpose," "united in spirit" (2:2).

The style of 2:5-11 is liturgical. The "form of God" is contrasted with "the form of a bond-servant" (1:6-8). The movement is from deity to humanity, from eternity to time and back to eternity.

The imperatives of 2:1-5 are grounded in the indicatives of 2:6-11.

Historical

Paul demonstrates his strong ties to the Philippians, using himself as a ground for exhortation: "Make my joy complete" (2:2).

Theological

The exhortation to unity begins by assuming the resources of "encouragement in Christ," "consolation of love," "fellowship of the Spirit," and "affection and compassion" (2:1). Here it appears that Paul mixes divine and human potentials. The "encouragement in Christ" refers to our eschatological hope, Christ's return and our triumph with Him. The "fellowship of the

Spirit" designates our present union with Christ, the power which that gives us, and the assurance that our hope will be realized. "Love," "affection," and "compassion" are all human attributes that produce unity.

This, however, is artificial. Whatever human potentials there are for love, affection, and compassion, these are only realized in Christ. It is Christ that purifies this potential and gives it the strength to endure even against suffering and rejection.

What we have then in Christ will be expressed in "the same mind," a common attitude, "the same love," a common affection and being "intent on one purpose," a common goal. The old life of "selfishness and conceit," where we must defend our position against others by putting them down, will give way to humility, our lowering ourselves to exalt others. Our preoccupation will not be with ourselves but with those about us (2:3), since Christ frees us from being the center of our own lives. All of this (2:1-5) is stated as exhortation leading into one of the classic New Testament passages on the person and work of Christ.

Paul introduces Christ's example as the ground for his call to unity and humility. The "one mind" (1:27) or the "same mind" (2:2) is the mind or attitude of Christ Jesus (2:5). This attitude is expressed by the movement from renunciation (2:6,7), to humiliation (2:7,8), to exaltation (2:9-11).

The Apostle begins by clearly asserting the deity of Christ. He was "in the form of God" (2:6). As such He gave concrete expression to the very nature of God. God's form is seen in Christ as the Father makes Himself known in the Son. This is analogous to John's proclamation of Jesus as the "Word of God," God's self-expression or communication to us (see John 1:1,2, 14). The unknowable God reveals himself in Christ.

Christ, however, did not grasp or hold on to His

equality with God (Phil. 2:6). Unlike Adam, He did not seek His own autonomy. He willingly gave up His position in heaven, emptying Himself of His rights, "taking the form of a bond-servant" (2:7). This renunciation meant His humiliation—He now expressed His divine nature as a slave, born as man (2:7). The divine form then was united to the human form (2:8). Both deity and humanity reside in Christ and are expressed through Him. When we see Jesus we see God and man simultaneously.

Since the expression of His humanity came in service (2:7), this meant humility and obedience (2:8). Jesus shows us our proper position before God. Our freedom is to serve. Our exaltation is our humiliation. Our destiny is fulfilled, living in obedience to the Father's will. All of this Jesus has revealed in His incarnate life.

The ultimate expression of Christ's humiliation is seen in obedience "to the point of death, even death on a cross" (2:8). The Son was free from His own rights, His own self-exertion, so that He was willing to die the death of a criminal, abandoned on execution hill.

Because of His fulfilling the Father's will, God has highly exalted Him (2:9). Christ now has the supreme name in all of creation—that of Lord (2:11). When the name of Jesus is heard, ultimately, every knee shall bow and every tongue confess His dignity bringing glory to the Father. Those who love Him will bow in joy. Those who hate Him will bow in fear. Whatever the motivation may be, all creation will be unified in the confession, "Jesus Christ is Lord" (2:11).

Here, then, the Apostle teaches the deity and the humanity of Christ. He also teaches the lordship of Christ over all creation. At the same time, Paul gives us a model for our own humanity. We are fulfilled as we renounce our rights and live in humble obedience to the Father. Christ is both the motive and the model for our life in the world and our life together. To have the attitude of Christ (2:2,5) means to follow His attitude to renunciation and humiliation. We must then trust God for our exaltation in His time.

Tactical

Not only are the Philippians faced with persecution from without but also with division from within. This becomes concrete in 4:2. Now, however, the Apostle engages in general exhortation to unity, giving it both a personal and theological ground. First, there is Paul's own appeal: "Make my joy complete" (2:2). Then there is the mind or attitude of Christ. This attitude, when made real through the Spirit, releases encouragement, love, affection and compassion (2:1). For the sake of Paul and Christ the Philippians are to recover a stance of humility in their fellowship with each other.

Contemporary

The world demands power, a powerful church to compete with or to balance its power. The value of the church is measured in its holdings. This reflects itself also in the demand for a "powerful" Christian life. There are those, in the words of Dr. James Mallory, who seek always to live "in the middle of a miracle."

The offense of Christ is that He shows Himself to the world in powerlessness. He comes not to compete with our pride but to break it. The means? Humility, servanthood, obedience to the Father's will.

The Jews demanded a Messiah of power; God delivered His Messiah to death. What a scandal! And yet what truth! Violence breeds violence. Hate breeds hate. Pride breeds pride. Christ comes, not to reinforce our pride but to expose it. He does this by washing our feet. Now we are undone. The great God of the universe—in Christ renouncing His rights. How can we claim ours before Him humbling Himself? How can we parade and strut into His presence? Our vicious circle of pride is broken by the humility of Christ, and we must bow before Him. Out of His humility and our humbling He is now proclaimed Lord of the universe. His name is above every name; God has highly exalted Him.

Where in the world do we see the reigning Lord? Not in a powerful Christian or a powerful church. But in a heart humbled before Him. Only Christ can break us and in our brokenness His Lordship is now seen. At this the world marvels. It can no longer demand that we play the power game on its terms. Christ has seized the terms on His knees, dangling from the cross.

Personal

I struggle for the mind of Christ. My insecurities position me as judge against other brethren. The devil tempts me to exalt myself in my spiritual position, my authority in Christ. My pride demands its rights. I seek the honored seat. I boil when slighted. My efforts demand recognition. My accomplishments form my identity. I want physical possessions to demonstrate my success.

Jesus comes in humility. He serves me. "What can I do for you?" He asks. Again I am undone.

What do the academic degrees mean staring blindly at me from my walls? What do my possessions say? They neither hear nor speak nor love. Today's honor is tomorrow's faded memory. All that is exalted in this world will be laid low. Christ, humbled in this world, is alone exalted.

He takes my hand and lifts me up. He sets me free to serve. He shows His power through my weakness. But I fight it. Then again I hear His name and my knee bows and my tongue confesses: He is Lord. When I am truly living with Jesus I am truly alive. How stupid I am to try any other life. "Lord, set me free to bow before you and confess your Lordship by serving this world again today."

INDUCTIVE QUESTIONS FOR PHILIPPIANS 2:12,13

12 So then, my beloved, just as you have always obeyed, not as in my presence only, but now much more in my absence, work out your salvation with fear and trembling;

13 for it is God who is at work in you, both to will and to work for His good pleasure.

Language

a. *Vocabulary: salvation*—the gift of God's acceptance in Christ.

b. *Style:* Paul reaches a conclusion, "So then," based on 2:1-11. He addresses the church with warmth, "my beloved." The contrasts here are between Paul's presence and absence and between the Philippians' work and God's work. These are both a command and a promise.

Historical

Paul asserts that he has previously been with the Philippians, although he is now absent. When he was with them, they obeyed his commands, in fact, they have always obeyed (2:12).

Theological

These verses have occasioned some confusion. Does Paul teach here that we are to work for our salvation? Is not this a contradiction of the gospel of God's grace?

Notice that there is a decisive difference between working "for" something and working "out" something. When I am working *for* a reward, it is in the future; it will be given on the basis of my effort. When I work *out* a math problem it is in the present, given by the teacher.

Salvation is God's gift. When I am set free from the penalty and power of sin, then I become responsible to live out this salvation—to grow and mature in my Christian life. All is by God's initiative but I also have response-ability. The resources are given for growth: the Holy Spirit, prayer, the Word of God, the sacraments, other Christians; but am I availing myself of them?

This freedom given in the gospel, this responsibility, causes an awe, a reaction in me of "fear and trembling." God entrusts me with salvation, now I must develop my Christian life and He will hold me responsible for the results (see 2 Cor. 5:10). Will I freeze in fear? No, Paul rushes in with the other side: "For it is God who is at work in you, both to will and to work for His good pleasure" (Phil. 2:13).

My freedom is in Christ, not away from Christ. God does not save me to abandon me. He gives what He commands (Augustine). He calls me to work out my salvation and then works in me to bring it about.

On the final day we will not congratulate each other upon our Christian accomplishment. All glory will be given to Christ; God has worked in us for His good pleasure. We will join all of heaven in giving the praise, honor and blessing to our God who is all in all.

Tactical

Paul's appeal to unity (2:1-11) means responsibility (2:12,13). The Philippians are not to be smug in their salvation. They are to realize it in demonstrating their unity in Christ. They are to press on with the confidence of God's work in them.

Contemporary

Part of the church calls us to massive human effort and neglects the grace of God. Part of the church calls us to the grace of God and neglects human effort. The Bible holds the balance.

We are responsible to live out the claims of Christ in the world. Non-Christians demand to see our faith, not just to hear about it. The old adage: "If you were arrested for being a Christian, would there be enough evidence to convict you?" has force. Where have we shown our care for the poor, minority groups, political corruption, the environment? The world and the liberal church insist upon such a demonstration, and they are right.

At the same time, human effort and idealism without the power of God are folly. We quickly exhaust our resources when our efforts are rejected or when change does not come overnight. How will we stand against the powers of evil? A generation who went to the south to help the blacks or who demanded our withdrawal from Vietnam was quickly disillusioned. Only when we know that God is at work in us "both to will and work for His good pleasure" can we endure beyond our own strength.

God's work in us will also keep our focus central. We will confess with Paul: "For to me, to live is Christ" (1:21). We will not become submerged in side issues. Our evangelical heart will continue to beat and all that we do will endure to eternity.

Personal

Early in my Christian life my whole focus was on salvation. My concern was getting people to heaven and going there myself.

As my education and experience broadened beyond a white middle-class community, I became aware of the tragedy and turmoil of our nation.

Living in New York City was a depressing experience for me. I looked at Harlem from Morningside Heights and saw a sea of black faces, trapped in unemployment and poverty. I came out of a subway staircase in the

119

dead of winter to find a man lying unconscious on the street. I walked Broadway listening to the desperate babblings of people lost in the haze of their removal from reality. I took bums to dinner rather than surrendering a quarter for cheap wine.

These experiences slowly became a call—a call to work out my salvation, not only in inner piety but also in obedient service.

As a pastor in Hollywood there would be a stream of black students from New York to be helped with their education in California. The Salt Company Coffee House would lead to crash pads, a job program, and long days and nights with hurting, alienated people.

If I really love a person the most loving thing I can do is to introduce him to Christ. But there are many other loving things I must do in the name of Christ. The Word must become flesh in me.

INDUCTIVE QUESTIONS FOR PHILIPPIANS 2:14-18

14 Do all things without grumbling or disputing;

15 that you may prove yourselves to be blameless and innocent, children of God above reproach in the midst of a crooked and perverse generation, among whom you appear as lights in the world,

16 holding fast the word of life, so that in the day of Christ I may have cause to glory because I did not run in vain nor toil in vain.

17 But even if I am being poured out as a drink offering upon the sacrifice and service of your faith, I rejoice and share my joy with you all.

18 And you to, I urge you, rejoice in the same way and share your joy with me.

Language

a. *Vocabulary: blameless*—see 1:10; *innocent*—without moral failure; *crooked*—dishonest; perverse, morally reprobate; "the *word of life*"—the gospel; *the day of Christ* see 1:6.

b. *Style:* Paul continues his exhortation: "Do all things . . ." (2:14), "and you too, I urge you, rejoice" (2:18). Several images appear. Christians are to shine as an Olympic torch, holding up the gospel (2:15,16). Paul runs as an athlete and labors as a worker in his ministry to the Philippians (2:16). The sacrificial language of worship is used in 2:17 to describe possible martyrdom.

Historical

Paul's pride is in the Philippians' witness and maturity (2:16). He may indeed die in the cause of Christ (2:17). If so, they should rejoice with him in this honor (2:18).

Theological

Paul has commanded the Philippians to work out their salvation promising them God's power and purpose: "For it is God who is at work in you" (2:13). Thus they are not now to grumble or question His will (2:14). When understanding fails, faith triumphs.

The result of this submission will be holy living in the midst of a "crooked and perverse generation" (2:15). Thus holiness is a result not of moral effort, but the submission to the will of God. Holiness is not a result of a holy environment (monasticism), but it is lived out in an evil environment in the world.

It is in the darkness that the light is seen most clearly. Christians "shine" as the will of God is manifest in their behavior. In this the "word of life" is visual as well as vocal. It is held fast as a torch lights the darkness (2:16).

The Philippians' holy living will fulfill Paul's ministry when Christ returns (2:16). By their faithfulness Paul's work will be seen as true.

If the Apostle is to die before the Lord comes, however, it will be a sacrifice on the behalf of the Philippians' faith (2:17). Since Paul's life is for Christ, his death will be for Christ (1:21). Thus both he and they are to rejoice (2:17,18). Their joy, on the one hand, is from the completion of Paul's desire to be with Christ (1:23). Paul's joy, on the other hand, is in their steadfastness and the privilege of his suffering for Christ even unto death (3:10).

Tactical

The themes of persecution and unity now climax in the Philippians' submission to God's will and Paul's joy at Christ's coming or in his martyrdom for Christ. The Apostle's death cannot quench his or the church's gladness and rejoicing. This is to be found in fulfilling the Father's will and accomplishing the goal He has set for Paul. The time of termination is in His hands.

Contemporary

Joy in suffering is always the Christian paradox. In the flesh we are gripped by the same fears of pain and the unknown as is any person of the world. In the Spirit, however, we are given a promise: Christ will be with us in the ultimate hour. We go *through* the valley of the shadow of death (see Ps. 23:4); we do not stay there (Raymond Lindquist). It is Christ's presence, even in death, which is the ultimate source of our joy. This the world cannot know or understand; it is the unique experience of the Christian.

My father-in-law, Duncan Rimmer, lay dying of cancer. At 52 this terminal illness was cruel. His healthy body wasted to skin and bones. As I gripped his hand, he said to me, "Don, I am on the verge of the greatest adventure of my life." The doctors and nurses around him were strangely drawn to this spirited man. In the pain there was the joy of Christ's presence and the promise of seeing Him face to face. How we die tests how we have lived. This is our final witness to the world. As Pope John XXIII said, "My bags are packed; I'm ready to go."

Personal

When Christ returns, Paul sees his converts as his witness to a faithful life for the Lord. The Apostle is not satisfied merely to win people to the faith. It is the quality of their Christian life and their steadfastness in the world that will be his "cause to glory" (2:16).

As I look over my life I think of how many people I have influenced to Christ and how few I now know are "above reproach" and "holding fast the word of life" (2:15,16). When time and space have separated us, I must entrust them to Christ. Where they are still within range, I must accept responsibility.

A young man, Bob Papazian, found Christ through our Coffee House in Hollywood. We were friends, he becoming the manager of our musical group, "The Salt Company." Over a three-year period we lost touch. Bob had legitimate bitterness toward me because of my failure to respond to his need when his father died. Then at a wedding we were again face to face. I spoke to him of Christ. We followed up with a luncheon meeting. I asked Bob to forgive me for letting him down in the past. Our fellowship restored, we now have breakfast weekly to share our lives and pray together. In the day of Christ, Bob's mature manhood in the Saviour will be my joy, his joy and Jesus' joy as well.

INDUCTIVE QUESTIONS FOR PHILIPPIANS 2:19-24

19   But I hope in the Lord Jesus to send Timothy to you shortly, so that I also may be encouraged when I learn of your condition.

20   For I have no one else of kindred spirit who will

genuinely be concerned for your welfare.

21   For they all seek after their own interests, not those of Christ Jesus.

22   But you know of his proven worth that he served with me in the furtherance of the gospel like a child serving his father.

23   Therefore I hope to send him immediately, as soon as I see how things go with me;

24   and I trust in the Lord that I myself also shall be coming shortly.

Language

Style: Turning to personal news Paul commends Timothy to the church. Notice the father-son image. Paul is the spiritual father of Timothy. Timothy shows his sonship by embodying the character of Paul.

Historical

To aid the Philippians in their crisis Paul writes this letter, dispatches Timothy and plans to visit the church upon his release. It will be through his and Timothy's presence that the church will be stabilized and encouraged. Paul does not leave this to a letter.

We also see here how Paul operates; he disciples Timothy as a son in the faith. By living with the Apostle, Timothy has learned the Christian life. Now he is an extension of Paul, able to respond to the crisis in his absence. Thus the ministry is extended and passed on to the next generation.

Timothy is unique to Paul; Paul has no one like him (2:20,21). Here Timothy receives the greatest compliment.

Theological

Paul has spiritual sons. He is the vehicle of the Holy Spirit through whom people are brought to Christ and nurtured in their faith. God chooses to use people for such tasks. This is our dignity and our responsibility.

Paul accepts his fatherhood—to provide for his children and to help them grow up into Christ. He knows that they will learn by imitating his life (3:17).

The results in Timothy have been rewarding. Timothy is free from selfish preoccupation; he genuinely cares for the Philippians. He now is a servant of Christ (1:1). Paul can exhort to humility (2:1-11) and send Timothy because he will live out what the Apostle teaches.

The principle is that of the Incarnation: the Word becomes flesh in us. It is through each other that the reality of the Christian life is to be seen.

Tactical

Timothy will reinforce Paul's teaching to the Philippians. He will represent Paul. He is commended warmly to the church to secure his open reception. The Apostle also plans to come. Thus the church is comforted and encouraged. Paul not only writes, he acts. Both his and Timothy's lives are on the line for this church.

Contemporary

Within the massive Christian education structures of our churches where is the place for the personal? We may teach or attend large classes, but who is Paul to us? Where is our father, investing his life into our lives? In turn, who is our Timothy? To whom are we committed to pray with, to study with, to live with and thus to mature in the faith?

The answer is not more Sunday School materials, visual aids, or teacher-training classes. The answer is a life invested in lives. In an impersonal world the church cannot afford to be impersonal. We are not a religious supermarket. As Coleman's book (*The Master Plan of Evangelism*) shows, Jesus' method was 12 men, not the multitudes. Has God changed His strategy today?

Personal

The model for my life as a Bible teacher is Earl Palmer, presently the pastor of the First Presbyterian Church in Berkeley, California. Earl was in seminary across the street from my college, and I followed him around for two years, as Timothy followed Paul.

When Earl taught, I was in the front row absorbing his words. When Earl went to a conference I went with him, learning by observation and imitation.

As I began to speak I sounded like Earl. When people noticed, I was embarrassed. But then I realized that this is the biblical principle. We learn in a living relationship; I was free to admit Earl's impact on my life.

As the years passed I developed more of my own theology and style and became my own person. Yet I will always thank God for the *molding* influence Earl had upon my life. Earl loved the Bible; I love the Bible. Earl cared for people; I care for people. This is the way I grew.

INDUCTIVE QUESTIONS FOR PHILIPPIANS 2:25-30

25 *But I thought it necessary to send to you Epaphroditus, my brother and fellow-worker and fellow-soldier, who is also your messenger and minister to my need;*

26 *because he was longing for you all and was distressed because you had heard that he was sick.*

27 *For indeed he was sick to the point of death, but God had mercy on him, and not on him only but also on me, lest I should have sorrow upon sorrow.*

28 *Therefore I have sent him all the more eagerly in order that when you see him again you may rejoice and I may be less concerned about you.*

29   *Therefore receive him in the Lord with all joy, and hold men like him in high regard;*

30   *because he came close to death for the work of Christ, risking his life to complete what was deficient in your service to me.*

Language

a. *Vocabulary: Epaphroditus*—a member of the church at Philippi who brought the church's gift of money to Paul in prison.
b. *Style:* The personal tone of 2:19-24 continues. Notice the titles Paul gives to Epaphroditus: "brother," "fellow-worker," "fellow-soldier," "messenger" and "minister" (2:25). The elaboration is for emphasis and commendation.

Historical

The Philippians responded to Paul's distress by dispatching Epaphroditus with a gift of money for him. Epaphroditus was both "messenger," he brought news of the church, and "minister," he served the Apostle's needs (2:25). Along the way, apparently he fell ill and the news went back to Philippi (2:26). Close to death, he nevertheless recovered, sparing Paul grief (2:27). Now the Apostle returns him to Philippi with strong commendation (2:25) and the request for him to be honored since he risked his life "for the work of Christ" (2:30). The Philippians' joy at Epaphroditus's return will bring relief to Paul (2:28).

Theological

Epaphroditus was apparently a "layman," yet Paul uses terms of equality in describing him: "brother," "fellow-worker" and "fellow-soldier." For the Apostle those about him stand side by side in the Christian mission. While conscious of his own apostolic authority,

Paul is delighted to elevate his companions, consider them equals and share with them the glory of Christ's call and work.

These titles are suggestive of Paul's understanding of his mission. "Brother," of course, represents the reality that by faith we are all adopted into God's family through Christ (see Gal. 4:5). Formerly orphans, now we belong in Christ. While there are distinctions of office, there are no distinctions of privilege, "For you are all one in Christ Jesus" (Gal. 3:28). The higher the office, the more is service expected: "If any one wants to be first, he shall be last of all, and servant of all" (Mark 9:35).

"Fellow-worker" expresses common partnership in a task. Paul works side by side with Epaphroditus. To the Corinthians the Apostle speaks of laying a foundation "as a wise masterbuilder" (1 Cor. 3:10). Now others join in the project, working on the base laid by Paul. This is an extended image for Paul's apostolic mission which is shared by others as they mature his churches. Epaphroditus is one of those laborers, working beside Paul to complete the growth of the Philippians.

At the same time, the Christian mission includes both upbuilding the church and battling the world. Thus Epaphroditus is also a "fellow-soldier" (2:25). Here Paul pictures himself at war. As he tells the Corinthians, "We do not war according to the flesh, for the weapons of our warfare are not of the flesh, but divinely powerful for the destruction of fortresses" (2 Cor. 10:3,4). Standing with him in the conflict, Epaphroditus has proven himself a true companion of Paul. War tests faithfulness. Epaphroditus has passed that test.

Thus in these titles we see both Paul's generosity and his genuine vision for the Christian life. Out of our family responsibility we are to upbuild the church and engage the world. This is the totality of Christ's call.

Tactical

In returning Epaphroditus to Philippi Paul sends encouragement to the church. Epaphroditus will also be able to reinforce the points made in the letter, interpreting the Apostle's meaning and preparing the Philippians for Timothy's arrival. Paul's strong endorsement (2:25, 29,30) will strengthen his hand as he too extends the Apostle's personal ministry through his warm association with Paul.

Contemporary

A major issue in the institutional church today is the gulf between clergy and laity.

Ministers often feel manipulated and intimidated. They face crises in roles, identity, and function. Underpaid and underappreciated, many men are leaving the pulpit.

At the same time, the laity often feel the aloofness of the clergy. How can they understand the personal and moral conflicts of the business world? What do the clergy know of sexual temptation, price-fixing, and unfair competition? How sensitive can they be to the spiritual deadness of life in the world with its constant compromise? What can they understand of family conflicts? How can a pastor be sympathetic to the problems of single men and women or the issues of women's rights? So the list grows.

The New Testament knew nothing of this professional gulf. The average congregation met in a home under lay leadership. The professionals made infrequent visits. At the same time, their humanness was not veiled behind a false piety. Paul's openness about his own struggles (see 2 Cor. 1:8ff.; Gal. 4:19,20) created openness among his converts. Paul's wide heart insured the love and trust of the Philippians.

In the Apostle's commendation of Epaphroditus (2:

25) we see the model for supportive relationships and functions between clergy and laity in the Body of Christ. This kind of sharing and caring will close the gulf and open the doors to renewal in local congregations.

Personal

I have often feared the laymen in my church. I fear their control of money. What big giver must I not offend? I fear their judgment on my work. How can I guarantee success and approval? I fear their gifts. What if some layman proves a better evangelist or preacher than myself? The result of this too often is aloofness on my part. I also fear not having much to talk about. What do I know of the world they face? What do they know of the theology I read?

A word from Dale Bruner comes to mind: "The most interesting person is the most interested person." No longer do I feel that I must maintain my professional dignity and position. No longer do I need to have all the answers. Now I too can come with my fears, struggles, and doubts. Where I am uninformed I can learn. Honest questions will open people up. When I genuinely care about a person I can enter his or her world and find a warm welcome.

Suddenly I discover many an Epaphroditus along the way—a brother, fellow-worker and fellow-soldier.

INDUCTIVE QUESTIONS FOR PHILIPPIANS 3:1

Finally, my brethren, rejoice in the Lord. To write the same things again is no trouble to me, and it is a safeguard for you.

Language

a. *Vocabulary: finally*—literal meaning, "now turning to exhortation."
b. *Style:* Imperative, exhortation.

Historical

"The same things" Paul writes could refer either to a previous letter or to that contained in chapters 1 and 2 or 3:2ff. The call to rejoice echoes from 1:18,19; 2:17,18.

Theological

Paul has spoken of his joy in prayer (1:4) and his rejoicing in the proclamation of Christ (1:18). At the same time, he rejoices in the prayers of the Philippians and his anticipated release from prison (1:19) which will bring reunion with them (1:25).

The Philippians' unity will also bring joy to Paul as the attitude of Christ is exhibited through them (2:2). The Apostle will rejoice if he is sacrificed for the church as he shares Christ's suffering. The church will rejoice in the completion of Paul's goal to be with Christ (2:17,18), as we have already seen.

All of this shows that joy comes from the presence of God (often in prayer). Rejoicing is the result of seeing God's purpose fulfilled whether it is in preaching the gospel, demonstrating divine unity, or departing to be with Christ.

Here then, Paul calls again: "rejoice in the Lord." Find your joy in his presence. Rejoice in His will. To repeat this exhortation is always timely.

Tactical

It is joy in the Lord that prepares the Philippians to contend for the faith in 3:2-21.

Contemporary

Where does joy come from? What do we have to rejoice about? Our joy in this world comes from relationships. This is good, even wonderful, and yet unsatisfying because no relationship can be sustained forever. Ultimate joy is in the presence of the Lord.

Our rejoicing comes from recognition, accomplishment, success. We conquer a task, fulfill a goal. We graduate from college, are hired for a job, marry the person of our dreams. In this we legitimately rejoice. And yet this gladness fades too. What can make us rejoice for eternity? Only the fulfillment of God's will. "Finally, my brethren, rejoice in the Lord."

Personal

I have had pure joy in the presence of another person. The night my wife told me for the first time, that she loved me, like Romeo, I dashed away from my balcony scene in ecstasy.

I have rejoiced in accomplishment. I recall climbing the steps of Lowe Library at Columbia University to submit the necessary copies of my approved doctoral dissertation. As the clock chimed four I descended those stairs with an overwhelming sense of fulfillment and relief. Years of labor were ended.

There is another more lasting joy—the night Christ entered my life and the reality of His presence that has never left. There is a deeper rejoicing than any accomplishment, seeing God work His purpose through my life and knowing that the results are eternal.

Rejoice in human relationships and accomplishments, yes. But, above all, rejoice in the Lord!

INDUCTIVE QUESTIONS FOR PHILIPPIANS 3:2-11

2 *Beware of the dogs, beware of the evil workers, beware of the false circumcision;*

3 *for we are the true circumcision, who worship in the Spirit of God and glory in Christ Jesus and put no confidence in the flesh,*

4 *although I myself might have confidence even in the flesh. If anyone else has a mind to put confidence in the flesh, I far more:*

132

5 circumcised the eighth day, of the nation of Israel, of the tribe of Benjamin, a Hebrew of Hebrews, as to the Law, a Pharisee;

6 as to zeal, a persecutor of the church, as to the righteousness which is in the Law, found blameless.

7 But whatever things were gain to me, those things I have counted as loss for the sake of Christ.

8 More than that, I count all things to be loss in view of the surpassing value of knowing Christ Jesus my Lord, for whom I have suffered the loss of all things, and count them but rubbish in order that I may gain Christ,

9 and may be found in Him, not having a righteousness of my own derived from the Law, but that which is through faith in Christ, the righteousness which comes from God on the basis of faith,

10 that I may know Him, and the power of His resurrection and the fellowship of His sufferings, being conformed to His death;

11 in order that I may attain to the resurrection from among the dead.

Language

a. *Vocabulary: dogs*—an epithet used against the Gentiles by the Jews; *evil workers*—a term denoting the opposite of the Jewish claim that the law creates "good workers"; *circumcision*—the Jewish sign of the covenant carved into the male sex organ (see Gen. 17:9-14); *the flesh*—living on one's own resources, depending on one's self rather than God; *the tribe of Benjamin*—one of the 12 tribes of Israel, the tribe from which King Saul came, thus the regal tribe; *Pharisee*—that school of legal interpretation which dominated first-century Judaism. The Pharisees had a rigor for the law and were careful in their piety and fidelity. At the same time, they created elasticity in their interpretations, redefining the law for new situations. Jesus constantly challenged them for their hypocrisy. *Righteousness*—here defined in two ways: (1) legal righteousness through human effort (3:6), and (2) God's gift of righteousness given through faith in Christ (3:9). Righteousness means a life lived in conformity to the law of God which yields His judgment of "not guilty." *Faith*—trust, surrender, the means of receiving God's gift of righteousness; *resurrection*—raising the dead, first Christ, and then those who believe in Him.

b. *Style:* The passage begins with exhortation as warning (3:2). This is based then in Paul's experience (3:4ff.). Thus the autobiographical style is seen in the use of "I." The structure is broken into "before" and "after" (3:7-11). Notice the use of superlatives: "I far more" (3:4), "blameless" (3:6), "the surpassing value" (3:8). The style is absolute which makes the contrast clear. The shift in emphasis is from Paul in the first part of the paragraph to Christ in the second. The Apostle uses repetition to build his case for his conversion: "For the sake of Christ" (3:7), for "the surpassing value of knowing Christ Jesus my Lord" (3:8), "that I may gain Christ" (3:8), "that I may know Him" (3:10).

Historical

Paul tells us that the church is endangered by legalists who would bring it under a performance religion. He describes them as "dogs," "evil workers," and "the false circumcision." This profanity is a sarcastic response to their legalistic claim. They turn out to be "dogs," as the Jews called the Gentiles in disdain. They are "evil workers" rather than "good workers" in seeking to impose the law. When circumcising their converts, they do so falsely.

Throughout his ministry, the Apostle was harassed by

Jewish-Christians who held that Gentiles must accept the Old Testament law to be true or complete believers (see Galatians). Here then is another example of such opposition which now endangers his gospel and work in Philippi.

In dealing with the legalists, Paul gives us a classic description of his own life before and after Christ. He substantiates the evidence we read about in the book of Acts for his Jewish past where he is represented as raised an orthodox, pious Jew. Not only did he have the proper credentials in ritual (circumcision) and race (tribe of Benjamin), but he followed the teaching of the Pharisees and acted out his faith in blameless moral behavior, with zealous persecution of heretics (3:6).

This passage reveals that Paul was not on the fringes of Jewish life, dissatisfied and ripe for conversion. Rather, he views himself at the cultural heart of Judaism. The Apostle was no revolutionary student, he was not a member of a disenfranchised minority; he was a moral, religious, zealous Jew with everything to gain by remaining such. Thus psychological and sociological explanations of his conversion crash on the rock of his own testimony. Far from feeling dissatisfied with the law, Paul viewed himself as "blameless" (3:6). Far from feeling guilty over his persecution of the Christians, Paul gloried in such a credential (3:6). It was all of this gain, then, that was surrendered for Christ (3:7). Paul gave up ritual, religion, morality, position, and his identity in Judaism, for "the surpassing value of knowing Christ Jesus my Lord" (3:8).

Theological

Paul defines religion clearly here. It includes proper acts ("circumcision") and proper ethics ("blameless"). For the Jews, it also includes proper blood ("a Hebrew of Hebrews"). All of this was abandoned when the

135

Apostle was met by Christ. The heart of evangelical faith is now revealed. Paul had a great system in Judaism and he exchanged it for a person. All of the merit of his works was shattered on the Damascus road. Religion as man's attempt to please God, to justify himself before God, was also shattered. Jesus Christ broke the system, revealing Himself as a person, and claimed Paul's life.

The result was that the Apostle moved from religion to a relationship, from performance to a person. Now it became the passion of his heart to simply "know Christ" (3:8). All of his past glory in Judaism was revalued as "rubbish" or "dung" (3:8, *KJV*).

What did Paul receive from this encounter? Firstly, a new *righteousness* (3:9). No longer did he have to perform for God's "Not guilty." Now he was accepted in Christ's right-standing with God. The acceptance given the Son by the Father was shared by Paul. He exchanged legal righteousness for gift righteousness; active righteousness for passive righteousness (Luther).

Secondly, Paul found a new *power*—the power that raised Jesus from the dead, the power of the Spirit, now dwelt in him (see Rom. 8:11). Having been accepted in the *position* of righteous before God through Christ, he now knew the *power* of God's presence in his life (Phil. 3:10). Here was a power to serve God, to keep the law, unknown in Judaism. Here was resurrection power; it literally raised the dead.

Thirdly, Paul now shared in Christ's *sufferings*. The persecutor became the persecuted. Rather than lamenting this, the Apostle found through suffering a deeper fellowship with the Lord who also suffered. This is the Christian surprise, joy in suffering (1:29). These sufferings were undoubtedly physical, but they were also emotional, mental, and spiritual. The deepest agony of Jesus on the cross was not the nails, it was the burden of sin and alienation from the Father which He bore.

Fourthly, this suffering may well lead to a *death* like Christ's at the hands of Roman law: "Being conformed to His death" (3:10). If to know Christ means to die with Him, then Paul is ready for that eventuality. Again, even a martyr's death is revalued in Christ.

Fifthly, Paul anticipates *resurrection* (3:11). The great goal of the Apostle's life is resurrection—the goal already accomplished by his Lord.

What we now see in this passage is that the example of Christ, the mind of Christ in 2:5-11, has become Paul's. As Christ renounced His position with God, so the Apostle renounces his position in Judaism. As Christ lived in humility and obedience, so the Apostle suffers in this world. As Christ has been exalted before the Father, so the Apostle anticipates that all will end in resurrection for him too. What Christ has done *for* Paul, He has done *in* Paul. This is the final argument against performance religion.

Tactical

In 3:2, Paul shows his continuing conflict with the Judaizers or legalists who would subvert the church by placing these young Christians under the Old Testament law.

The Apostle demonstrates the stupidity of this by proving that true religion is spiritual not carnal (3:3). Performance can only create a false security and a secret pride. Over against this, the "true circumcision" worships God and glories in Christ, *not* in itself.

To make his case, Paul appeals to his own experience. If anyone kept the law, he did. If anyone should go to heaven for zeal or piety, he should. But now, knowing Christ, the Apostle has surrendered all of his glory and views it as "dung," "rubbish" (3:8). He abhors what he loved, and renounces it for life with Christ in His righteousness.

Against the legalists, Paul claims, *I tried it, I did it; I even did it with more zeal and success than you ever could or will, and it failed.* To the church he says, *Learn from my experience, my example.* In the words of an old Packard commercial, "Ask the man who owns one."

Contemporary

The church is gripped by performance religion. While we preach a gospel of justification by faith, we live a gospel of justification by works. We reward the righteous. We manipulate people to perform properly in their "Sunday best." We presume that all good Christians will act a certain way and support our programs. Thus we create tests for righteousness, expecting a cultural conformity from each other, and thus practically deny God's gift of righteousness in Christ.

How easily the camels of works-righteousness possess the tent. This battle must be refought in every generation, in every church, in every heart.

The powerlessness of much of today's church comes from unbelief. We do not really believe that Christ proclaims us righteous by faith. Thus we struggle to achieve our own standing before God. This cuts off the ground of our power and our suffering for Him which are the signs of Christ's righteousness (3:9,10). A powerless church is also a church without persecution. Living on our own strength means we are living like the world. No wonder we fit in so well.

At the same time, the living person of Christ is displaced by religion—theology, liturgy and ethics. In Karl Barth's insight, "Religion is man's last defense against the living God." True faith in Christ will issue in a good theology, vital liturgy and a moral life. But these results can never replace the person. Where faith dies, the form remains, becoming an end in itself. No wonder many of our churches stand under the judgment of God. Perfor-

138

mance or a person, religion or a relationship; these alternatives must be thrust home as never before.

Personal

I grew up in a liberal protestant church. I was taught the Fatherhood of God, the brotherhood of man, and my basic goodness. I was taught that God loved good boys who were kind to their pets, obedient to their parents, and went to church. God was a giant Santa Claus who would fill my socks with blessing when I was good. I became bored and dropped out of religion.

Even at 15 years of age, my questions were not those of the liberal church. I felt alienated and guilty. I feared death. I longed for some purpose in life and I was deeply and basically lonely.

Here Christ met me in caring people who loved Him and loved me and in true preaching which announced Him as alive and which called me to live in Him.

In a moment of prayer and surrender, Christ became a person to me; my old life—"rubbish," my new life—Christ. Paul's witness is my witness—to "know Him." Nothing else matters. Either Christ speaks, or there is only ultimate silence in the universe and our day leads irrevocably to endless night.

INDUCTIVE QUESTIONS FOR PHILIPPIANS 3:12-16

12 Not that I have already obtained it, or have already become perfect, but I press on in order that I may lay hold of that for which also I was laid hold of by Christ Jesus.

13 Brethren, I do not regard myself as having laid hold of it yet; but one thing I do: forgetting what lies behind and reaching forward to what lies ahead,

14 I press on toward the goal for the prize of the upward call of God in Christ Jesus.

15 Let us therefore, as many as are perfect, have this

attitude; and if in anything you have a different attitude, God will reveal that also to you;

16   *however, let us keep living by that same standard to which we have attained.*

Language
a. *Vocabulary: perfect*—sinless, mature or complete.
b. *Style:* The personal exhortation continues. Paul contrasts a negative and a positive in 3:12 and 3:13,14. Notice the repetition for emphasis: "I press on" (3:12,14). Notice also the metaphor of a race from the Olympic Games in 3:13,14.

Historical
It is possible that Paul warns here against those who would claim that Christians are already "perfect," that the Resurrection is a spiritual event rather than an historical event (3:12). This, however, is not certain.

He does assume that there are some in Philippi who are "perfect" and agree, with him, that they are not already perfect (3:12).

Theological
In one verse, Paul expresses his responsibility and Christ's sovereignty. Having not yet arrived, the Apostle presses on toward the resurrection because Christ has claimed his life (3:12). It is natural for us to see ourselves first, our tasks, our challenge ("I press on"), but then we see that all that we have is from Christ, and in this we rest ("in order that I may lay hold of that for which also I was laid hold of by Christ Jesus").

Again in 3:13 Paul restates the contrast for emphasis. Paul has not yet attained his goal, but rather than wallowing in his guilt, he presses on: "Forgetting what lies behind and reaching forward to what lies ahead, I press on . . . " (3:13,14).

140

Like an athlete, the Apostle's eyes are on the prize (3:14). Toward this he strains (3:13). The goal is God's upward call in Christ (3:14). To achieve this, to be resurrected with Christ, to enter heaven to be with Christ in glory—for all of this Paul strains in the race of faith. Those who are perfect are to run with him trusting God for the future (3:15).

From this paragraph we learn again the forward-stance of the Christian life. We are to look back to Christ's work with thanksgiving. We are to look up to Christ with confidence. But we are to move forward to Christ for the consummation of our call. Our life is to be lived eschatologically—toward the future. We press on because Christ has claimed us (3:12). We press on because the goal is clear, and God has called us to it (3:14). The Christian life is no smug arrival, no presumptuous victory. It is pressing on to the final end when with Christ all will be fulfilled.

Tactical

If indeed there are those in Philippi who hold themselves to have arrived, this paragraph is a telling rebuke. At the same time, it completes Paul's own witness. Knowing that Christ has called him and made him His own, the Apostle does not presume on this; he presses on. Rather than legal performance for acceptance, now having been accepted, Paul "performs" to complete his calling, knowing that Christ is at work in him. Now there is a new motivation: it is a person, Christ, and the fulfillment of His will.

Contemporary

There are those today among Christians who confuse justification and sanctification. Justification describes my position before God as "not guilty," resting in Christ's righteousness (3:9). Sanctification describes the process by which I become subjectively what I already am objectively. Sanctification is "pressing on." In this passage, Paul rebukes those who claim to have arrived, those who hold that all has been fulfilled for them. No, the call is to go on. But we go on to what we already have—to the Christ who has come and who is coming. In that call we realize the full potential given when we say yes to Christ.

Paul also defines our call as "upward" (3:14). We are called beyond our sin, beyond temptation, beyond the fear and failure and death of this world. This raises the question of goals. What is worthy of our lives?

There are many answers, some are personal (success, money, power); some are ideological (the dictatorship of the proletariat, the Third Reich, making the world safe for democracy). The problem with our goals in this world is that they are not "upward." They are neither elevating nor eternal. Our personal and ideological goals are trapped by the finitude, sin, and corruption of this world. We are trapped by our selfishness.

Christ comes with an "upward" call. We are called out of ourselves to Him. We are called out of ourselves to each other. We are called to move through time to eternity. It is this "upward" call that is alone worthy of us because we have been made for it. To settle for less is counterfeit.

Personal

Paul writes, "But one thing I do" (3:13). I write, "These thousand things I do." How can the Apostle be so goal-oriented? How can he reduce his life to one thing?

In reflection on the text, I realize that Paul did not simply *do* one thing. He did many things; his letter to the Philippians makes this clear. But he did many things for one person: Jesus Christ (1:21). It was Christ who integrated Paul's life. Thus it is Christ who can knit the fragments of my life together and hold me with one central purpose and direction.

Does this mean that as a Christian I do not pay taxes, feed my dog, shop for groceries, or drive to work? Absurd! It does mean, however, that all I do is to be for Christ. He holds it all together. He puts the mark of eternity upon it. Christ integrates my life into one thing: "And whatever you do in word or deed, do all in the name of the Lord Jesus, giving thanks through Him to God the Father" (Col. 3:17).

INDUCTIVE QUESTIONS FOR PHILIPPIANS 3:17-21

17 Brethren, join in following my example, and observe those who walk according to the pattern you have in us.

18 For many walk, of whom I often told you, and now tell you even weeping, that they are enemies of the cross of Christ,

19 whose end is destruction, whose god is their appetite, and whose glory is in their shame, who set their minds on earthly things.

20 For our citizenship is in heaven, from which also we eagerly wait for a Savior, the Lord Jesus Christ;

21 who will transform the body of our humble state into conformity with the body of His glory, by the exertion of the power that He has even to subject all things to Himself.

Language
a. *Vocabulary: the cross of Christ*—the gospel; *citizenship*— identity, belonging.
b. *Style:* Exhortation.

Historical
The Philippians are tempted by legalism (3:1-11) and

license (3:17-21). Under pressure the Gentile Christians may revert to their old pagan ways.

Paul has often warned them of this, even weeping (3:18). He sorrows over those who find life fulfilled in the passing pleasure of the moment.

Theological

Paul offers a trenchant critique of the materialist. Firstly, end is destruction (3:19). Since all material things pass away, it is a foolish man who would find permanent meaning in that which is transitory. Secondly, materialism turns means into ends: "Whose god is their appetite" (3:19). The appetite, made to sustain life, is made into life. A small god, indeed. Thirdly, by placing ultimate value in the lower, the materialist reveals his own inferiority: "Whose glory is in their shame, who set their minds on earthly things" (3:19). Our pilgrimage is to prepare us for heaven; it can never be heaven. Thus the materialist, having locked God out of his universe (deism) or having identified God with his universe (pantheism), ends up losing everything as this world passes away.

Over against this, Paul offers the heavenly world (3:20). There is our identity, our citizenship. There is our security. Our end is not the materialist's destruction, but a Saviour, Jesus Christ, and the transformation of the temporal into the eternal (3:20,21). We have two choices: disintegration or transformation. Since Christ has risen from the dead, our transformation is certain: He "will transform the body of our humble state into conformity with the body of His glory" (3:21). This is our answer to materialism. It is the answer of the risen Christ.

Tactical

Paul is facing the false alternatives to the Christian

144

life—legalism and license. To those in danger of reversion to the old life the Apostle contrasts earth with heaven, the material with the spiritual. It is the Lord who subjects all things to Himself (3:21).

Contemporary

We hardly need to go beyond the obvious in applying this text to our culture. We live in a nation drunk with materialism. The experiences of recession and economic dislocation have jolted some. Most, however, naively go on their way. "Consume, consume, consume," is our motto. We measure success by acquisition. We turn means into ends. All culminates in destruction.

The church apes the world. Our spiritual success is measured in budget and buildings. But the end is destruction. Into a materialistic world the gospel comes with penetration and insight. The world passes away; without eternity time becomes absurd.

The east (Buddhism, Hinduism) offers a false spirituality which is the denial of the material, annihilation. But if God is the creator we cannot renounce His creation.

Christ offers a true spirituality: transformation. The material will be released from bondage and decay. The risen Christ will transform our lives and our world and deliver all from the curse of disintegration and death. We thank God for the material and see in it the sign of the spiritual. Both material and spiritual are fused in Christ: "The Word became flesh" (John 1:14). Here the spiritual triumphs not over the material but in the material. Here God is ultimately seen as the transformer. He who subjects "all things to Himself" (Phil. 3:21).

Personal

My temptations are to wallow in my material being or to escape into my spiritual being. Christ holds the two together.

At times, I have despaired of my body like a good Greek. I have been so frustrated, so tempted, so embattled that I am ready to denounce my body.

At other times, I have been so caught up in the Spirit, so removed from the physical that again I am ready to denounce my body.

Christ holds my body and spirit together. A sign of this for me has been the gift of marriage. In my single state sex frustrated me so that I was tempted to indulge its demands or deny its reality in spiritual euphoria.

When God gave me a Christian wife, I could accept my sexuality as good and yet not be trapped by it. Some of the best times physically in marriage have also been the best times spiritually.

I can now accept my physical nature and yet look beyond it to the Saviour who will bring transformation in my conformation to Himself.

INDUCTIVE QUESTIONS FOR PHILIPPIANS 4:1

Therefore, my beloved brethren whom I long to see, my joy and crown, so stand firm in the Lord, my beloved.

Language
a. *Vocabulary: crown*—the reward in an athletic contest, symbolizing reward at the return of Christ (see 1 Thess. 2:19).
b. *Style:* Exhortation based upon personal motivation. Notice the terms Paul applies to the Philippians, "brethren" and "beloved."

Historical
Paul longs for the Philippians, to be present with them.

Theological
The Apostle's call is for the church to "stand firm."

The Philippians are to be firm in their faith and firm in their loyalty to Paul. He in turn addresses them as his "brethren" and his "beloved." He loves them and longs for them. They will be his joy and crown when Christ returns.

Here again, we see Paul's boldness in drawing these Christians emotionally to himself. He uses the language of love with passionate abandon. While perhaps offensive to some, the Apostle indicates here again that he is a vehicle of Christ's love to the church. How will we know of the reality of that love? By Christians who become channels through which we are drenched.

Tactical

Paul now calls the church to stand firm against the false alternatives of legalism and license, based upon the Philippians' loyalty and affection for him and he for them.

Contemporary

The call to "stand firm" echoes emptily through a church which has surrendered the substance of the faith to a relativistic age. "Stand firm in what?" we ask. How can we stand firm in the confusion of denominations and the cacophony of theologies? The answer? "Stand firm thus in the Lord." It is Christ Himself who transcends all of the relativities of our age. He stands in judgment upon our denominational pride. He judges our theological speculation. We can only stand firm in the Lord because only the Lord stands above finitude, transitoriness, sin and presumption. We stand firm in Christ —the Eternal One—or we do not stand at all.

Personal

I have sought to stand firm in many places. I have sought security in my family, my education, my vocation, my friends. All have given me some disappointment. I have sought to stand firm in myself—the ultimate folly. As Rick Nelson's "Garden Party" puts it, "I learned my lesson well. If you can't please everyone, then you might as well please yourself." But I can't even please myself. I let me down. I forsake my own morals, ideals and values. All of this comes as the gentle teaching of Christ—He loves me and drives me to Himself. Here, at last, is the rock. Here alone, I stand firm.

INDUCTIVE QUESTIONS FOR PHILIPPIANS 4:2,3

2   *I urge Euodia and I urge Syntyche to live in harmony in the Lord.*

3   *Indeed, true comrade, I ask you also to help these women who have shared my struggle in the cause of the gospel, together with Clement also, and the rest of my fellow-workers, whose names are in the book of life.*

Language

a. *Vocabulary: Euodia* and *Syntyche*—women leaders in the church of Philippi who are now the cause of the division Paul addressed in 1:27—2:11. Paul identifies them as equals in ministry (4:3). *True comrade*—an unknown helper in the church whom Paul hopes to be a mediator between Euodia and Syntyche; *Clement*—another leader among the Philippians.

b. *Style:* The exhortation becomes pointed and personal as Paul calls the resources of the church into play to heal its division.

Historical

Euodia and Syntyche are women whom Paul names as the sources of division in the church. At the same time, they have been co-laborers in the gospel with Paul, Clement, and other fellow-workers (4:3). Apparently, the division is over personalities or perhaps methods, but not the gospel or matters of theology. If it were the latter, Paul would speak directly to such substantial issues.

The Apostle shows us here that he accepted women equally in his ministry ("These women who have shared my struggle in the cause of the gospel," 4:3) and that they could thus cause a rift in the church.

"True comrade," a title for an unknown leader, is to help in the reconciliation of these women (4:3).

Theological

The place of women in the church is a hot issue today. Here we can only speak to the positive evidence. This must be compared with other letters.

Paul tells us in passing that Euodia and Syntyche were equal co-laborers in his ministry in Philippi (4:3). They are also placed beside, not under, Clement, a male, and "the rest of my fellow-workers" (4:3).

Their labor or struggle was "in the cause of the gospel" (4:3). Thus they shared in the spiritual, evangelical ministry which was Paul's.

Achieving positions of leadership, these women could split the church, evoking some of Paul's highest Christological proclamation (2:5-11).

If women are not in similar positions in our churches today, our congregations cannot be held to be Pauline. When the Apostle writes that in Christ there is neither male nor female (see Gal. 3:28), he apparently lived this out in providing leadership for the early Christian communities.

The ultimate reconciliation in Christ and equality before Christ is to be lived out in the church. This is a challenge to our congregations today.

Tactical

Paul now confronts the sources of division. He dealt

149

with them generally in 1:27—2:11 and now specifically in 4:2,3. He marshalls the resources of the congregation to aid in the reunion of Euodia and Syntyche.

Contemporary

The Women's Liberation Movement has much to say to the world and to the church. Women are discriminated against in our culture. They are "things," objects of male lust. They are valued for their bodies not their minds. They are exploited financially. They are stereotyped as valuable only for the bedroom and the kitchen. They are forced into roles which have nothing to do with their creation in the image of God (see Gen. 1:27).

Too often, the church has spiritualized cultural roles and blessed them with the sanctity of the clergy. Women have been largely powerless in major denominations. Lacking financial muscle, they have been excluded from the boards of the church. Lacking seminary education, they have also been refused ordination. As this is being written, these conditions have changed only slightly since the increase in activities in the women's rights movement.

In this passage, Paul demonstrates the value and position of women in the church. He places them upon equal footing with himself, "fellow-workers" (4:3).

We must survey our own congregations. Where is Euodia? Where is Syntyche? Both God and the world await our answer.

Personal

It is easy for me to look down upon women in spiritual things. Often I find myself "turning them off." The voice of man carries greater authority.

Yet, the person who built the great Sunday School at Hollywood Presbyterian Church was a woman. Henrietta Mears worked as director of Christian education at the Hollywood church and at the same time founded Gospel Light Press and Forest Home Christian Conference Center. Her influence for Christ has been felt around the world.

If God could use Miss Mears, God can use any woman. The gifts of the Spirit are not given with sexual discrimination. The next woman to speak with me may bear the word of God. Will I hear?

INDUCTIVE QUESTIONS FOR PHILIPPIANS 4:4-7

4 *Rejoice in the Lord always; again I will say, rejoice!*

5 *Let your forbearing spirit be known to all men. The Lord is near.*

6 *Be anxious for nothing, but in everything by prayer and supplication with thanksgiving let your requests be made known to God.*

7 *And the peace of God, which surpasses all comprehension, shall guard your hearts and your minds in Christ Jesus.*

Language

a. *Vocabulary: rejoice*—see 4:4; *the peace of God*—a sense of wholeness coming from unity with God.

b. *Style:* Exhortation.

Historical

Theological

Rejoicing in the Lord comes from the confidence that His purpose is to be fulfilled, "The Lord is near" (4:5). Because of this we are able to forbear, to endure.

This confidence relieves anxiety about the future (4:6). This is the *motive* for release. The *method* is prayer: "In everything by prayer and supplication with thanksgiving let your requests be made known to God" (4:6).

Our needs and problems are to be named before God, in "prayer and supplication"—(4:6). As we bring them to Him we are to have "thanksgiving" (4:6). This comes from the assurance that He hears us, lifts the burden and answers. There can be no anxiety where there is thanksgiving. When we are truly thankful, we are released.

Of course we rarely fully realize this. Too often we commit our way to the Lord only to take it back, or we struggle with our doubts and fears. The promise stands, however, and the result Paul promises is peace (4:7). God's acceptance will guard us in both thought and emotion as we release ourselves to Him. This "surpasses all comprehension" because it is not a mental process, the "power of positive thinking"; it is God's gift, pure and simple.

Tactical

The division threatening the church through Euodia and Syntyche will only be healed as their problems are released to the Lord. Thus Paul's call to reconciliation is not only a call to human aid (4:3), it is a call to prayer (4:4-7).

Contemporary

For persons who have endured emotional illness, who have suffered acute anxiety attacks, these verses sound cheap. Paul seems to offer a spiritual Band-Aid rather than radical surgery.

At the same time, these verses stand. If God does not will our emotional distress, then to rest and rejoice in Him must bring freedom. The process, however, is often a long one. Where we have emotional wounds, fractured relationships and disappointments, trust will not come easily. Where God seems to have disappointed us, prayer will be a chore. Where bitterness fills us, thanksgiving will be empty. As we are healed, however, in helping relationships, as the Body of Christ loves us and is Christ to us, the potential of taking these verses as they stand will reappear.

Two dangers must be avoided: (1) *a cheap theology* which clubs people to silence with verses such as these, never allowing them to share their disappointments and hurts; (2)*that unbelief* which denies the powerful truth held here.

God is working His purpose out. We rejoice. He is coming for us. Prayer is our release to Him. Thanksgiving heals our bitterness and disappointment. God's peace floods us in the unexpected moment. I trust Him not because I fully understand but because He is trustworthy.

Personal

I have seen Christians dear to me fall apart under the pressures of modern life. Through this I have come to appreciate the healing power of psychiatry, especially when practiced by a believer.

All of us have emotional blocks and repressions which need to be removed. When they become unmanageable, we need professional help. Such help, however, has its limits. I can experience emotional healing and be spiritually dead. I can experience spiritual life and be emotionally disturbed.

Paul gives a formula here for health. My ability to entrust my life to God spiritually will rest in part on my emotional resources. If these are lacking I need help. This help can come directly through divine intervention. I have seen such healings where disturbed, drug-possessed youth have been delivered by Christ. This help can come indirectly through medical help. I have seen people emerge from therapy, able again to trust God. Christ is Lord of the process whether it be long or short. Christ is Lord of the results. Final healing is always spiritual. Here prayer is the means, peace the result. This I have found in my own life.

INDUCTIVE QUESTIONS FOR PHILIPPIANS 4:8,9

8 *Finally, brethren, whatever is true, whatever is honorable, whatever is right, whatever is pure, whatever is lovely, whatever is of good repute, if there is any excellence and if anything worthy of praise, let your mind dwell on these things.*

9 *The things you have learned and received and heard and seen in me, practice these things; and the God of peace shall be with you.*

Language
a. *Vocabulary: Finally*—see 3:1.
b. *Style:* Substantial and personal exhortation.

Historical
Paul offers his life again as the model for what it means to live as a Christian (4:9; 3:17).

Theological
The peace of God comes through prayer and is sustained as our minds dwell on the truth of God. This is described here in general terms as that which is "true," "honorable," "right," "pure," "lovely," and "good repute." If we were to define these words abstractly it would be a great error. All of these values have been baptized into Christ. The truth is in Jesus. Honor is found in Him. He alone grants what is right. Purity is His person. He is "altogether lovely." Good repute is found in Him.

Thus as we pray (4:4-7) our minds are drawn to the character of God revealed in Jesus (4:8). There we are to rest, we are to "dwell on these things."

The character of God becomes concrete now in Paul.

154

Thus the immediate transition to the Apostle's example is made where these virtues are to be seen (4:9).

God's truth is always incarnate. This is the way we learn. A living Christian models the reality to which we are called. For the Philippians, this is Paul.

Tactical

Unity will be realized in prayer (4:4-7) and sustained as the Philippians focus on the character of Christ as exhibited in the life-style of Paul (4:8,9).

Contemporary

Paul can offer his life as the example of all that is found in Christ (4:9). If the Philippians follow him, the God of peace will be with them. This appears to be presumption, yet the Apostle is certain that Christ lives in him and works through him (see Gal. 2:20).

Too often we rely on other than living Christian examples to build up the church. We call the roll of the saints, but we deny living saints in our midst.

We fear that if people really knew us the work of Christ would be destroyed. Yet Paul expects the Philippians to see Jesus in him.

It is exactly when we are open and vulnerable that people are able to distinguish between our sinfulness and Christ. When they see our weaknesses they will know Christ's strengths (see 2 Cor. 12:9).

People are constantly crying out for the kind of caring leadership from the church that will say: "The things you have learned and received and heard and seen in me, practice." Dare we get so close to people, so involved with them that we can say this? It will only be so by the grace of God.

Personal

The peace of God comes as a result of prayer (4:7) and

the God of peace is with us as we follow the lives of mature Christians (4:9). Here Paul holds together the spiritual and the historical.

I advance in my Christian life as I have fellowship with Christ and with His people. One cannot exclude the other. At times I have attempted to grow only by prayer and Bible reading. I have tried to cultivate spirituality alone. At other times I have dived into people, largely abandoning personal spiritual discipline. Both responses are one-sided. I need my personal walk with Christ; I need the example and encouragement of fellow Christians. I am to live with Christ and my brother. The promised result is the peace of God. So, Lord, let it be!

INDUCTIVE QUESTIONS FOR PHILIPPIANS 4:10-13

10 But I rejoiced in the Lord greatly, that now at last you have revived your concern for me; indeed, you were concerned before, but you lacked opportunity.

11 Not that I speak from want; for I have learned to be content in whatever circumstances I am.

12 I know how to get along with humble means, and I also know how to live in prosperity; in any and every circumstance I have learned the secret of being filled and going hungry, both of having abundance and suffering need.

13 I can do all things through Him who strengthens me.

Language
a. *Vocabulary: rejoice*—see 3:1.
b. *Style:* Personal witness. Notice the frequency of "I."

Historical
The Philippians have sent money to Paul. We learn later that this is a continuation of their previous support

(4:14-20). His imprisonment created a new opportunity for them.

While the Apostle is thankful for their help (4:10), he does not really need it. He is content regardless of his circumstances (4:11,12).

Theological

Coming to the conclusion of his letter, Paul now summarizes the point made in 1:12-26. He is no prisoner of his circumstances. He can handle any external state. He can deal with wealth and poverty, plenty and hunger. The key to Paul's life is neither in the world nor in himself; it is in Christ (4:13).

Christ strengthens Paul for the battle. Christ is the secret of his triumph. Christ goes through all adversity with him. Christ makes up for his weakness. Christ comforts him in loss and humbles him in gain. Since life is in Christ (1:21), Paul is a genuinely free man.

There are two realities and they are simple. First of all, Christ gives him His presence. Second, Christ gives him His strength (4:13), and these are enough. Satisfaction for Paul and for us will only be found here: "I can do all things through Him who strengthens me" (4:13).

Tactical

The Apostle turns now specifically to thank the church for the gift of money and at the same time he concludes the letter. On the one hand he appreciates their help. On the other hand he did not need it. Christ is the secret of his life, and this thesis for the letter (1:21) is also its conclusion.

Contemporary

Paul speaks here of the secret to all the changes of life; it is to be grounded in the changeless person of Christ. In one sense it is easier to be abased than to abound.

When we are in trouble, facing adversity, we find it easy to call upon the Lord. Our foxhole makes us people of faith. When we abound, however, we easily rely upon ourselves. Prosperity deludes us into assuming that we don't need Christ. When money talks, God is often silent. What danger! How easily it all crashes in upon us.

Yet, Paul has a word for an affluent society, Christ makes me able to abound. I can handle money when Christ handles me.

My success is translated into responsibility for the Lord. I see through the delusion of trusting in material success or personal power. Pascal speaks of Christ as the one who makes small things great and great things small. In Him I can be abased and abound.

Personal

Trusting Christ in relative ease is a great struggle for me. When I was trying to revive a choking drug addict, prayer was spontaneous and natural. Living an ordinary life, however, can make the need for God's power distant. How can I deal with this? One answer is to push out again; not to let my material ease and security keep me from needy, hurting people. Another answer is to see how much I need God in each moment, how what He has given me must be used for His glory. The final answer is simply to keep Christ ever before me, to love Him, to praise Him, to allow Him to be my secret for life.

INDUCTIVE QUESTIONS FOR PHILIPPIANS 4:14-20

14   Nevertheless, you have done well to share with me in my affliction.

15   And you yourselves also know, Philippians, that at the first preaching of the gospel, after I departed from Macedonia, no church shared with me in the matter of giving and receiving but you alone;

16   for even in Thessalonica you sent a gift more than once for my needs.

17   Not that I seek the gift itself, but I seek for the profit which increases to your account.

18   But I have received everything in full, and have an abundance; I am amply supplied, having received from Epaphroditus what you have sent, a fragrant aroma, an acceptable sacrifice, well pleasing to God.

19   And my God shall supply all your needs according to His riches in glory in Christ Jesus.

20   Now to our God and Father be the glory forever and ever. Amen.

Language

a. *Vocabulary: Macedonia*—the northern province of Greece; *Thessalonica*—the capital city of Macedonia; *Epaphroditus*—see 2:25; *glory*—the character of God which evokes praise in us.

b. *Style:* Personal news (4:14-19) concluding with an ascription (4:20). Notice the image of worship in 4:18.

Historical

After their conversion the Philippians immediately aided Paul financially in his mission (4:15). They sent money to Thessalonica more than once (4:16), and continued their help even after that (4:15). Now, again, their support has come through Epaphroditus (4:18). Paul verifies that their messenger has delivered the full amount and, in effect, signs a receipt (4:18). For all of this the Apostle is warm and grateful (4:14,17,18,19). He builds giving congregations.

Theological

Paul sees the gift of money from the Philippians as an offering to God (4:18). Worship must include our material possessions or it is merely words. "Where your treasure is, there will your heart be also" (Matt. 6:21), our Lord tells us. If our heart is in heaven, there we will invest our treasure.

While the Philippians' gift went to Paul and aided him, it was given to God. As our lives are surrendered to Him our substance will support His work. As we give, so God gives: "And my God shall supply all your needs" (Phil. 4:19). As it is often said, "We can't outgive God." His promise is to meet our needs, not our luxuries. He has proven that promise in the gift of Christ. All His riches, all His glory are now ours. If we are a dead end in our giving, rather than an open channel, we become stagnant and corrupt. It is only to the giving that more will be given. This is the Bible's spiritual principle.

Tactical

Now Paul thanks the Philippians specifically for their money and offers his receipt. This is the appropriate and tactful conclusion. Their partnership (1:5) is demonstrated in giving. For this he salutes them and entrusts them to God.

Contemporary

Worship today is viewed as receiving rather than giving. We complain if the choir is off-key or the sermon dull. We attend church to be served. We wait for the action from up front.

Worship for Paul is giving. Israel had been taught to come to God with praise, prayer, and the offering of gifts. The ultimate offering is ourselves as "living sacrifices" (see Rom. 12:1,2). Thus when the Philippians send money and encouragement to Paul, they are engaging in worship—they are giving themselves away to God and to His work. Worship is just that concrete and just that vital.

True worship will always spring from such giving. As we give ourselves, God then can give to us (4:19). If we hold onto what we have, where will there be room for more?

Personal

Paul writes that he seeks not the gift but the fruit (4:17). Too often I have sought the gift. I have valued the wealthy, courted the big supporters of Christian work and looked upon as an end: "Why, if we just had more money ... "

But Paul sees the fruit. The fruit is, first of all, a generous heart in the giver. The fruit is, second of all, the work the gift does in spreading the gospel. When I see the fruit I realize again that giving is spiritual. My ministry in helping people to give is a spiritual ministry. Health and growth in Christ come in part through genuine giving. I need this ministry in my own heart and I need to extend this ministry to those about me.

INDUCTIVE QUESTIONS FOR PHILIPPIANS 4:21,22

21   Greet every saint in Christ Jesus. The brethren who are with me greet you.

22   All the saints greet you, especially those of Caesar's household.

Language

a. *Vocabulary: saint*—see 1:1; *Caesar's household*— those servants and administrators connected with the imperial palace, including the praetorian guard (1: 13).

b. *Style:* Farewell greetings. The key word is "greet" (4:21,22).

Historical

Paul is not alone; Timothy (1:1) and others are with

161

him (4:21). Some in the imperial household have become Christians through Paul's and others' witness (4:22).

Theological

Paul sends greetings to the church on behalf of the Roman Christians. In an alienated world the bonds of love crossed ancient barriers and unknown men and women formed God's new family. Thus they greeted each other in Christ.

We are also bound together in Christ. Our Christian greeting is to be given to the whole family, and we must stand behind it with our lives. These simple greetings are signs of the new work of the gospel in re-forming human relationship.

Tactical

Standard greetings are given binding the churches together.

Contemporary

We fail to greet each other in the church when we are separated by tradition, liturgy and theology. Out of our fears we hide or pass by with pleasantries.

Paul greets "saints" and "brethren"; those who have been called out of the world into Christ's family. If we view each other as such we will greet each other accordingly.

Personal

I am often separated from others by traditional divisions. When I was speaking recently at a college in Minnesota, a young black student stopped me and asked me about my views of the sacrament and apostolic succession. He was obviously Roman Catholic. As we talked, I tried to show him that while these theological questions were important, the real question was Jesus Christ and my relationship to Him. At this he lit up. He had found Christ in a Baptist church and was now heading for the priesthood. While accepting his traditional Catholic theology, he had a life-changing experience of the grace of God. We were brothers and embraced as such. We gave a common greeting in the Lord, and that bond transcended 500 years of separation and division.

INDUCTIVE QUESTIONS FOR PHILIPPIANS 4:23

23   *The grace of the Lord Jesus Christ be with your spirit.*

Language
a. *Vocabulary: grace—see 1:2.*
b. *Style:* Benediction.

Historical

Theological
This letter begins in grace (1:2) and ends in grace. All that has been done and all that will be done comes through Christ to us, freely given without reservation or qualification.

That grace is a spiritual reality. It meets our spirits, brings us into life, sustains and matures us, and prepares us for the day of Christ when we will be complete in Him (1:6). Paul leaves the Philippians where he finds them, in the grace of Christ.

Tactical
The answer to persecution, division and heresy is grace, and to that grace the church is now committed.

Contemporary
We trust our wisdom, our experience, our know-how.

American technology will succeed where all else fails. But what has this to do with the spirit? Only the Holy Spirit can minister to the spirit. Only the Spirit of Christ can bring grace, and without grace all else proves vain.

Personal

Can I leave people with the grace of Christ? When all is said, can I take hands off and trust God? What freedom is to be found there! For too long I have taken responsibility for others in a neurotic way. This has brought frantic effort and undue guilt. The answer? Grace, commending Christ's grace to those for whom I care, and leaving them in God's hands.

Part III

Study for Individuals and Small Groups

The studies in Part III have been prepared on several major passages in Philippians for individual and small-group use. They can serve as an excellent summary and review after you have completed the commentary. They also can be used simply by going to the biblical texts without prior study. The question form will guide you step by step.

Since these four studies focus on commitment, the person and work of Christ, the gospel, and the Christian life, they are ideal for young or new Christians. They can be pursued by small groups either with one leader or with a revolving leadership through the four sessions. Some of the studies, especially I and III, may take more than one small-group session to complete. Feel free to break them up into two meetings or more if necessary.

The studies give simple instructions and use questions to help you in thought and discussion. The creative student will use them as a springboard to further questions. Their purpose is to stimulate your own thinking and probing which is at the heart of inductive study. At the same time, you will be called upon to use your imagination and apply the text to your own life now. Study for Christian discipleship must never be abstract.

If you master these four studies you will have gripped the heart of the Christian faith, a solid foundation upon which you can continue your Christian life.

Write out your answers to each question and be prepared to share your responses with other Christians who would like to study the Word of God with you.

After the four studies you will find several memory verses which may be cut out of the book and carried with you. There is a great value in memorizing Scripture so that God's truth will become a substantial part of your life.

Review these verses in your spare time or before going to sleep. In a few days they will become a part of you. Learn the references, too. This will help you find them quickly and add authority when you share them with others.

SESSION I: COMMITMENT—PHILIPPIANS 1:12-26

1. Pray for God to give you an open heart for this session.
2. Read Philippians 1:12-18. Give immediate answers to these questions without a lot of pondering:
   a. Is there anything that you don't understand? What needs clarification?
   b. What major points does Paul make here? What are the themes of this passage?
   c. What *new* insights or thoughts strike you?
3. Recreate Paul's situation:
   a. Imagine the prison—what do you see? What do you hear? What do you smell?

b. Who is there with Paul? Imagine what these different people are like.

c. What does Paul do during the day?

4. Respond personally to what you see:

a. How would you react to arrest for being a Christian?

b. How could you spend your time in jail?

c. How do you think the Christians around you would respond to persecution for their faith?

5. Recreate the situation of the Christians on the outside of the prison (1:14-18):

a. Who are the other Christians?

b. What different motives do they have for evangelism?

c. Imagine these different groups. How do you picture them?

d. What difference is Paul's imprisonment making in their lives?

e. Why does Paul rejoice although some Christians oppose him?

6. Respond personally to what you see:

a. How can one person's example influence other lives? Where is one Christian making a difference in your world?

b. How do you deal with Christians whose motives you suspect?

7. Look back over 1:12-18:

a. How does Paul deal with his adverse circumstances?

b. Where are you facing adverse circumstances? Be specific. How have you dealt with them in the past? How can this passage help you face adverse circumstances now?

8. A thought to ponder: "If you were arrested for being a Christian would there be enough evidence to convict you?" What is the evidence in your life?

167

9. Read Philippians 1:19-26. Give immediate answers to these questions without a lot of pondering:
   a. Is there anything you don't understand? What needs clarification?
   b. What major points does Paul make here? What are the themes of this passage?
   c. What *new* insights or thoughts strike you?
10. Picture Paul's attitudes:
   a. What is his emotional state?
   b. What are his hopes and expectations?
   c. What are his conflicts?
   d. What is his central conviction or desire?
11. Respond personally to what you see:
   a. What is your central conviction or desire? Be honest.
   b. What difference does this make in your attitude toward death?
   c. What difference does this make in your attitude toward life?
   d. How can Paul's experience and witness help you?
12. A thought to ponder: "Paul can triumph over his circumstances because Christ has triumphed over Paul." Has Christ triumphed over you? Can you claim verse 21 as your own?
13. The Christian life begins in committing yourself to Christ. This means giving up your life into His hands. Have you made this commitment? If not, talk to Christ now and ask Him to take your life. If you have, then reaffirm your commitment and ask Christ to show you how to live it out today in the midst of your circumstances and relationships.

SESSION II: THE PERSON AND WORK OF JESUS CHRIST—PHILIPPIANS 2:1-11

1. Pray for God to give you an open heart for this session.

168

2. Read Philippians 2:1-4. Give immediate answers to these questions without a lot of pondering:
   a. Is there anything that you don't understand? What needs clarification?
   b. What major points does Paul make here? What are the themes of this passage?
   c. What *new* insights or thoughts strike you?
3. The issue behind this passage is division among Christians:
   a. What resources does Paul give for our being together (v. 1)?
   b. How are we to act so that unity is promoted among the Christian body?
   c. Describe the profile of the Christian that Paul pictures here.
4. Respond personally to what you see:
   a. Why do we have conflicts as Christians?
   b. When is conflict necessary and legitimate?
   c. When is conflict sinful and wrong?
   d. How do you handle conflict in the Christian body? How do you see others handling conflict around you?
5. A thought to ponder: "If you were not a Christian what practical difference would it make in your relationships with others?"
   Think over where Christ is making the difference in your family, among friends, teachers, and business associates. Be as specific as possible.
6. Read Philippians 2:5-11. Give immediate answers to these questions without a lot of pondering or concern about details:
   a. Is there anything here that you don't understand? What needs clarification?
   b. What major points does Paul make here? What are the themes of this passage?
   c. What *new* insights or thoughts strike you?

7. Describe the overall picture of Christ that Paul gives us:
   a. What two things do we learn about Christ from all eternity in verse 6?
   b. What did Christ surrender when He came into the world?
   c. List the several points which Paul makes about Christ's earthly life and ministry. Can you illustrate them from the four Gospels?
   d. Where is Christ now? What should our relationship be to Him now?
8. Reflect upon the question "Who is Jesus Christ?" How would you answer it from this passage?
9. Reflect upon the question "What has Jesus Christ done?" How would you answer it from this passage?
10. Respond personally to what you see:
   a. Why is it important to have a true picture of Jesus Christ? How will what we *know* influence what we *believe* and what we *do*?
   b. How did I picture Jesus before reading this passage? Has anything been added to my picture of Him now?
   c. How will my picture of Jesus affect my life? How will the "attitude of Christ" (v. 5) make a difference in the way I relate to others?
11. A thought to ponder: "Tell me what you believe about Jesus Christ and I will tell you who you are." How does Christ change my understanding of myself? How did I view myself before accepting Him? How do I view myself now?
12. Take some time to think over who Christ is and what He has done for you. Meditate on Him and then turn your meditation into prayer. Every knee will bow before Him. Every tongue will confess Him Lord. Now is your opportunity to share personally in worship and praise to the Lord Jesus Christ.

SESSION III: THE NATURE OF THE GOSPEL—
PHILIPPIANS 3:2-21

1. Pray for God to give you an open heart for this session.

2. Read Philippians 3:2-11. Give immediate answers to these questions without a lot of pondering:
   a. Is there anything that you don't understand? What needs clarification?
   b. What major points does Paul make here? What are the themes of this passage?
   c. What *new* insights or thoughts strike you?

3. The first false alternative to the gospel is legalism or performance religion:
   a. How does Paul describe performance religion in verses 2-6? As a Jew what did he have to boast about?
   b. Imagine Paul as a Jew. What do you see him doing?
   c. What did Paul find in Christianity that he did not have in Judaism?
   d. What two kinds of righteousness does Paul describe in verse 9?
   e. Imagine Paul as a Christian. What do you see him doing? How costly is his faith?

4. Respond personally to what you see:
   a. Where have you been involved in "performance religion"?
   b. As a Christian is this still an issue in your life? Is it an issue in the church today?
   c. Where does the pressure to perform for God's love come from?
   d. How do you identify with what Paul says about his relationship with Christ?
   e. How costly is your Christian commitment?

5. A thought to ponder: "Religion is man seeking God. Christianity is God seeking man." How does this

thought relate to Paul's own Christian experience?
How does it relate to yours?

6. Read Philippians 3:12-16. Give immediate answers
   to these question without a lot of pondering:
   a. Is there anything here that you don't understand?
      What needs clarification?
   b. What major points does Paul make here? What
      are the themes of this passage?
   c. What *new* insights or thoughts strike you?

7. The second false alternative to the gospel is perfec-
   tionism— the attempt to be perfect in this life:
   a. What picture does Paul give here of the Christian
      life? What does he deny? What does he affirm?
   b. What is Christ's responsibility?
   c. What is Paul's responsibility?
   d. When will we be perfect?

8. Respond personally to what you see. Imagine that
   you are running a race for Christ:
   a. Where are you in that race?
   b. What have you done with the past things in your
      life?
   c. What is the goal of your race?
   d. How do you see yourself running? What are your
      resources? What holds you back? What drives
      you on?

9. A thought to ponder: "It is Christ alone who is
   perfect, not us. We are free to be who we are today
   in Christ." How are you experiencing freedom in
   your Christian life?

10. Read Philippians 3:17-21. Give immediate answers
    to these questions without a lot of pondering:
    a. Is there anything that you don't understand?
       What needs clarification?
    b. What major points does Paul make here? What
       are the themes of this passage?
    c. What *new* insights or thoughts strike you?

11. The third false alternative to the gospel is materialism:
    a. Who are the enemies of the cross of Christ?
    b. What is Paul's attitude toward them?
    c. What is Paul's answer to them?
12. Respond personally to what you see:
    a. Where does materialism have a hold on your life?
    b. How often in each day are you told to consume something? How often are you told that material things will make you happy? Give examples.
    c. What is our proper response to this material world?
13. A thought to ponder: "Jesus Christ came to where we are to take us to where He is." How does this affect our understanding of the material world?
14. In light of Philippians 3 and the false alternatives to the gospel, make a positive statement as to what the gospel is and how it works in your life.

SESSION IV: THE CHRISTIAN LIFE— PHILIPPIANS 4:4-13

1. Pray for God to give you an open heart for this study.
2. Read Philippians 4:4-9. Give immediate answers to these questions without a lot of pondering:
    a. Is there anything here that you don't understand? What needs clarification?
    b. What major points does Paul make here? What are the themes of this passage?
    c. What *new* insights or thoughts strike you?
3. Paul exhorts us about the attitude of our spirits and the attitudes of our minds:
    a. How is prayer the key to spiritual peace?
    b. What elements of prayer are suggested here by Paul?
    c. What do you think of when you hear the words listed in verse 8?

    d. Why does Paul introduce his example in verse 9?
4. Respond personally to what you see:
    a. What role does prayer have in your life?
    b. What results do you see in praying?
    c. How does your "mind-set" affect your attitudes and growth?
    d. What role does the example of other Christians have in your life?
5. A thought to ponder: "Prayer is to the Christian life as breathing is to the body." Think over this analogy. How is it true for you? Another thought to ponder: "When we pray, it isn't so much that we change God, but that He changes us." How is this true for you?

A NOTE ON MEMORIZING BIBLE VERSES

We are told in Scripture the value of memorizing the Word of God. The psalmist writes, "Thy word have I treasured in my heart, that I may not sin against Thee" (Ps. 119:11). Paul tells Timothy, "All scripture is inspired by God and profitable for teaching, for reproof, for correction, for training in righteousness; that the man of God may be adequate, equipped for every good work" (2 Tim. 3:16,17). Jesus used the Word of God in defeating the temptations of the devil (see Matt. 4:1-11).

Thus our growth in Christ and our effectiveness in witnessing for Him will be strengthened as we memorize Scripture. Included in this study are 10 memory verses which can be cut out and carried with you. They will help you to master Philippians, share Christ with authority, think about excellent things (Phil. 4:8) and grow in the Lord.

Memory Verses

(From the *New American Standard Bible*)

1. Grace to you and peace from God our Father and the Lord Jesus Christ. Philippians 1:2	**2.** For I am confident of this very thing, that He who began a good work in you will perfect it until the day of Christ Jesus. Philippians 1:6
3. For to me, to live is Christ, and to die is gain. Philippians 1:21	**4.** For to you it has been granted for Christ's sake, not only to believe in Him, but also to suffer for His sake. Philippians 1:29
5. Do nothing from selfishness or empty conceit, but with humility of mind let each of you regard one another as more important than himself. Philippians 2:3	**6.** Have this attitude in yourselves which was also in Christ Jesus. Philippians 2:5
7. But whatever things were gain to me, those things I have counted as loss for the sake of Christ. Philippians 3:7	**8.** I press on toward the goal for the prize of the upward call of God in Christ Jesus. Philippians 3:14
9. Be anxious for nothing, but in everything by prayer and supplication with thanksgiving let your requests be made known to God. Philippians 4:6	**10.** I can do all things through Him who strengthens me. Philippians 4:13